D1547762

The Difference Engine

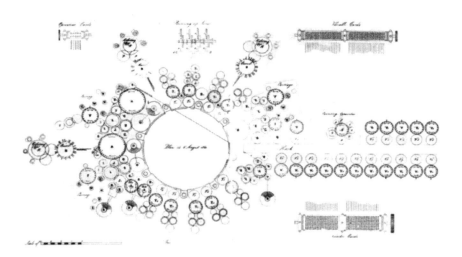

The Difference Engine

Computing, Knowledge, and the Transformation of Learning

Eugene F. Provenzo Jr.

ROWMAN & LITTLEFIELD PUBLISHERS, INC.
Lanham • Boulder • New York • Toronto • Plymouth, UK

Published by Rowman & Littlefield Publishers, Inc.
A wholly owned subsidiary of The Rowman & Littlefield Publishing Group, Inc.
4501 Forbes Boulevard, Suite 200, Lanham, Maryland 20706
www.rowman.com

Estover Road, Plymouth PL6 7PY, United Kingdom

British Library Cataloguing in Publication Information Available

Library of Congress Cataloging-in-Publication Data

Provenzo, Eugene F.
  The difference engine : computing, knowledge, and the transformation of learning /
Eugene F. Provenzo, Jr.
    p. cm.
  Includes bibliographical references and index.
  ISBN 978-1-4422-1435-4 (cloth : alk. paper)—ISBN 978-1-4422-1437-8 (ebook)
  1. Computers–Social aspects. 2. Computers and civilization. 3. Education–Effect of
technological innovations on. 4. Learning, Psychology of. I. Title.
  QA76.9.C66P77 2012
  303.48'34—dc23   2011046051

Printed in the United States of America

For Asterie,

Who has always believed in me and my work, with love and affection.

TABLE OF CONTENTS

Preface

Since the early 1960s the assumptions underlying culture and education have dramatically changed. So too has technology changed. The rapid evolution of media such as television and film, and in particular the computer, have created a new cultural geography—a "virtual geography."[1] This book is written as a conscious critique of the new landscape that is beginning to emerge as part of this geography—one whose terrain increasingly incorporates the computerization of contemporary culture and education. It is written by a technophile who realizes that we are at a critical moment in our culture—one where we are moving from a modern into a post-modern culture—from a Gutenberg and typographic model of literacy to a new post-typographic literacy. [2]

The words that dominate our cultural discussions and which will be found throughout this book—words such as Hypertext, Hypermedia, Hyperreality, Augmented Intelligence, Cyberspace, the Internet, the World Wide Web, Networked Knowledge, Collective Intelligence, the Information Superhigh¬way, Virtual Reality, Wikis and Mobile Computing—did not even exist a generation ago. Yet, the concepts that they represent are redefining the meaning of culture and society, education and literacy, learning and knowledge.

I am writing this book in part as an attempt to establish a dialogue with the cultural and educational establishment, but more specifically with those individuals who refer to themselves as critical and post-modern educational theorists. In particular, I am writing it with people such as Michael Apple, C. A. Bowers, Hank Bromley, Nicholas Burbules, Tom Callister, James Gee, Henry Giroux, Joe Kincheloe, Richard Kahn, Colin Lankshear, Jay Lemke, Allan Luke, Carmen Luke, Robert McClintock, Peter McLaren, William Pinar and John Willinsky in mind. I do so with respect for and interest in their work and the realization that with the exception of Bowers, Kahn, Lemke and Willinsky, and to some extent Apple, Bromely, Burbules, Callister, Gee, Lankshear, Lemke and Willinsky none of them have addressed the deep structural and cultural meaning of the computer for contemporary culture and education.

Bowers's work is particularly noteworthy. Drawing on the work of Don Idhe and, in turn, Martin Heidegger, his writing raises perhaps the single most important issue concerning computers and their use in our culture and educational system—the issue of their "non-neutrality." His work on computing, however, is largely ignored in the specialized literature on digital culture, as well as in the more general literature on education, culture and post-modernism.

The title for this book, *The Difference Engine*, is drawn from the name given by the early nineteenth-century English mathematician and economist Charles Babbage to his experimental calculating machine—"The Difference Engine."[3] Historians widely consider Babbage's machine (an extraordinary construction of machined gears and cogs) to be the first modern (albeit non-electronic) computer.

I have chosen this title because I want to create for the reader an image to describe the convergence of different aspects of contemporary computing, culture and literacy. These different aspects, or parts, while interesting and significant in and of themselves, combine together like the components of a complex machine—hence the metaphor of an engine. I am likewise drawn to the multiple meanings of the word "difference," in particular the idea of the machine as creating a condition or situation in which things are no longer the same. As with an engine, the different parts of the machine have their own separate operations and functions, but their real significance lies in their combined operation. My main tool for analyzing the engine and its parts is critical theory.

In order to understand how our culture and educational system are being transformed by the "The Difference Engine," I focus on seven of its main components: 1. Hypertext/Hypermedia—the eclectic combination of text, sound, graphics, animation, film and interactivity—that is the foundation of the new electronic literacy; 2. Augmented Intelligence—the use of computers by humans as ways of enhancing cognition; 3. Networked Information and Communication Systems—online services such as the Internet and the World Wide Web, which are creating a highly interconnected worldwide information network; 4. Collective Intelligence—the linking of people electronically through connected systems of thought, organization and action; 5. Hyperreality—Jean Baudrillard's notion that we are creating an increasingly electronically mediated culture in which simulations are no longer referential beings or substances, but the main reality of our lives and experience; 6. the Panoptic Sort—the collection of electronic data that allows individuals to be observed, regulated and controlled, and 7. Mobile computing—the use of computing in transit.

I am generally impressed by the potential of hypertext and hypermedia, convinced that augmented intelligence redefines us and our work as human beings, cautiously optimistic about the Internet and the World Wide Web, excited by the possibilities of sharing and community found in systems of networked knowledge and collective intelligence, intrigued and saddened by the culture of simulation and hyperreality, frightened by the panoptic sort, and intrigued by the possibilities and problems provided by mobile computing.

This book is consciously "Janusian" Like the bearded and two-faced ancient Roman god Janus (the god of doorways and beginnings), it looks both forwards and backwards at once. It draws heavily on historical comparisons from the Renaissance, as well as the seventeenth, eighteenth and nineteenth centuries. It also tries to anticipate trends involving contemporary technological developments and their potential cultural ramifications. It attempts to incorporate elements of post-modern literacy and consciousness, not only into its words, but into its design as well. In doing so, it attempts to return to some of the traditions and spirit of Humanist bookmakers and writers from the early Renaissance, while at the same time anticipating some of the possibilities provided to postmodern scholars by hypertext and hypermedia.

Eugene F. Provenzo, Jr.
University of Miami
Spring 2011

Notes

1. Critical Art Ensemble, *The Electronic Disturbance* (New York: Autonemedia, 1994), p. 3.

2. See the author's book: *Beyond the Gutenberg Galaxy: Microcomputers and the Emergence of Post-Typographic Culture* (New York: Teachers College Press, 1986) for a detailed discussion of the relationship between a typographic and post-typographic culture. Similar themes are also addressed by Ivan Illich in his work *In the Vineyard of the Text: A Commentary to Hugh's Didascalion* (Chicago: University of Chicago Press, 1993). In a similar context, it is worth noting that the word media as we know it is barely older, having been introduced into the language by Marshall McLuhan in the early 1960s. See Marshall McLuhan, *Understanding Media: The Digital Extensions of Man* (New York: Mentor Books, 1964). 30th anniversary edition with an introduction by Lewis Lapham (Cambridge: M.I.T. Press, 1994). Aslo see: C. A. Bowers, *The Cultural Dimensions of Educational Computing: Understanding the Non-Neutrality of Technology* (New York: Teachers College Press, 1980), and *Let Them Eat Data: How Computers Affect Education, Cultural Diversity, and the Prospects of Ecological Sustainability* (Athens: University of Georgia Press, 2000).

3. The Difference Engine was first conceived by the J. H. Müller, an engineer in the Hessian army in 1786. In 1822, the Englishman Charles Babbage, proposed the creation of such a machine to the Royal Astronomical Society. Babbage went on a few years later to design a more general calculating machine he named the Analytical Engine. In the late 1840s he produced a new machine his "Difference Engine No.2."

Acknowledgements

I wish to thank my wife Asterie Baker Provenzo, for her help on this project. Gary N. McCloskey, O.S.A., has been my student and friend, colleague. Our discussions about computers and their impact on contemporary education and society have been a pleasure and a constant source of new insights and ideas. Arlene Brett, Stephanie King, Chuck Mangrum, Jeanne Schumm and Bill Vilberg have helped me remember the reality of the classroom and how computers redefine the meaning of what it is to be a teacher. Alan Whitney, technology consultant extraordinaire, was always there when the "damn machine" wouldn't work. Beth Harry provides a supportive and sane environment in which to work, as does Dean Isaac Prilleltensky. Thanks to both of them.

Special thanks go to Phil Altbach and Lois Patten for suggesting that I write this book.

Lewis Wilkinson saved me from my self and technology on a number of occassions. Special thanks for his friendship and unselfish guidance and help. Thanks also to Alain Bengochea. He and Lewis know why.

Ray Firehock suggested a change of the title of the book at the last moment, one which I feel greatly improved its meaning. His insights and willingness to serve as a sounding board for new ideas is always appreciated.

Illustrations on pages 32 and 39 are reproduced with permission from Dover Books. Illustrations on pages 28, 37, 38, 40, 42, 54, 82, 137, 183 and 194 were made available from the Library of Congress. Mrs. Lillian Lewicki provided permission for the pictures on pages 68, 72, and 77.

Theresa Bramblett provided a last minute illustration for the dynabook. Many thanks for your lovely work and great sense of humor.

An earlier version of Chapter 6 was originally published as "The Electronic Panopticon: Censorship, Control and Indoctrination in a Post-Typographic Culture," in Myron Tuman, editor, Literacy Online: The Promise (and Peril) of Reading and Writing with Computers." Pittsburgh: University of Pittsburgh Press, 1992, pp. 167-178. Thanks go to the University of Pittsburgh Press for allowing it to be adapted for inclusion in this book.

Chapter 1

Introduction

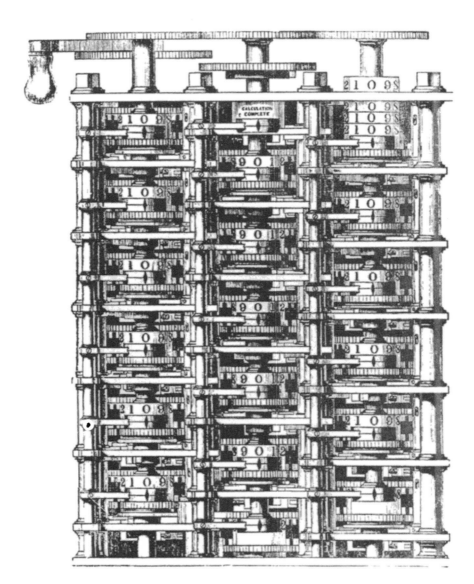

Frontispiece from Charles Babbage's *Passages from the Life of a Philosopher* published in 1864 showing a portion of his Difference Engine, which evolved from this earlier creation, the Analytical Engine.

This book assumes that the microcomputer revolution that began during the late 1970s and early 1980s has entered a second stage of development. It is one that involves six converging and closely related computer-based phenomenon: 1. *Hypertext/Hypermedia*, 2. *Augmented Cognition and Intelligence*, 3. *Networked Information and Communication Systems*, 4. *Collective Intelligence*, 5. *Hyperreality*, 6. the *Panoptic Sort*, and 7. *Mobile Computing*. Each of these computer technologies is part of a larger confluence of technologies in our society—and each is a part of what I call the "Difference Engine." In the following chapter, I will briefly introduce each of these concepts. Subsequent chapters look at them in more detail and reflect upon their significance for contemporary culture, computing ,and education.

Hypertext/Hypermedia

Hypertext, or "hypermedia," is not a new concept. Theodor Holm Nelson—the inventor of the term hypertext—notes in *Literary Machines*[1] that in 1945 the computer pioneer Vannevar Bush (1890-1974) described a publishing system called a "Memex."[2] According to Bush, the Memex would be:

> a sort of mechanized private file and library . . . a device in which an individual stores his books, records and communications, and which is mechanized so that it may be consulted with exceeding speed and flexibility. It is an enlarged intimate supplement to his memory.[3]

The Memex would be a desk-sized device. It would store massive amounts of microfilm so that "if the user inserted 5000 pages of material a day it would take him hundreds of years to fill the repository."[4] Most of the content of the Memex could be purchased on microfilm, ready for insertion into the machine. Books, pictures, periodicals and newspapers could be dropped into the system. Personal notes and materials could be entered as well. An index would be included that would allow the user easy navigation through the system: "A special button transfers him immediately to the first page of the index. Any given book of his library can thus be called up and consulted with far greater facility than if it were taken from a shelf. As he has several projection positions, he can leave one item in position while he calls up another."[5] Marginal notes could be added using a dry photography method.[6]

Bush envisioned the Memex providing an immediate step to "associative indexing," a system whereby, "any item may be caused at will to select immediately and automatically another."[7] Associative indexing would represent the essential feature of the Memex. Through it, items from different sources could be tied together or linked.[8] Bush explained, for example, how:

> The owner of the Memex, let us say, is interested in the origin and properties of the bow and arrow. Specifically he is studying how the short Turkish bow was apparently superior to the English long bow in the Crusades. He has dozens of possible pertinent books and articles in his Memex. First he runs through an encyclopedia, finds an interesting but sketchy article, leaves it projected. Next, in a history, he finds another pertinent item, and ties the two together. Thus he goes, building a trail of many items. Occasionally he inserts a comment of his own, either linking into the main trail or joining it by a side trail to a particular item. [9]

Bush believed that totally new types of encyclopedias could be created, which could be "dropped into the Memex and then amplified."[10]

A new type of scholarship could be realized using Bush's system in which a researcher would not only leave a record of his summations or interpretations, but also of the "trails" he had worked through in the documents included in the system. According to Bush:

> There is a new profession of trail blazers, those who find delight in the common record. The inheritance from the master becomes not only his additions to the world's record, but for his disciples the entire scaffolding by which they were erected.[11]

Bush was utopian in his outlook. He assumed that "man's spirit should be elevated if he can better review his shady past and analyze more completely and objectively his present problems."[12] The Memex would provide the necessary instrument by which to do this.

The Memex system was mechanically awkward—if not almost totally impractical. Conceptually, it was brilliant, anticipating to a remarkable degree the creation of hypertext and hypermedia, and even, as Chapter 4 will maintain, aspects of the Internet and the World Wide Web. The Memex is important conceptually because it is, in effect, a hypertext or hypermedia system.

Hypertext does not lend itself to a simple definition. Ted Nelson defines it as "*non-sequential writing*—text that allows choice to the reader, best read as an interactive screen."[13] Popularly conceived, this represents "a series of text chunks connected by links which offer the reader different pathways."[14] Nelson makes clear the inadequacy of this definition. Referring to hypermedia ("the amplification of hypertext that incorporates sound and visual material, links nonverbal as well as verbal information"), George Landow, a literary scholar, art historian and pioneer in the use of hypertext systems, explains that:

> The defining characteristics of this new information medium derive from its combination of blocks of text joined by electronic links, for this combination emphasizes multiple connections rather than linear reading or organization.[15]

Jeff Conklin describes hypertext as a system which makes possible "direct machine-supported references from one textual chunk to another; new interfaces provide the user with the ability to interact directly with these chunks and to establish new relationships between them." According to Conklin:

> The concept of hypertext is quite simple: Windows on the screen are associated with objects in a database and links are provided between these objects, both graphically (as labeled tokens) and in the database (as pointers).[16]

For Michael Joyce, hypertext, which he equates with hypermedia, is first and foremost a visual form, which embodies information and communications, artistic and affective constructs, and conceptual abstracts alike into symbolic structures made visible on a computer-controlled display.[17] It is a form, according to Joyce, in which print gives way to digitized sound, animation, video, virtual reality and computer networks or databases that are linked to it. Images can be "read" as though they are texts.[18] For Joyce, hypertext is "the revenge of the text on television since under its sway the screen becomes subject to the laws of syntax, allusion and association, which characterize written language."[19]

Norman Meyrowitz argues that hypertext is different things to different people. For some it is a means of teaching writing, for others it enables them to put encyclopedias and dictionaries online. Hypertext can be a system of argumentation and discourse, as well as a way of linking and connecting intellectual discussions and explorations. For others it is a vehicle for developing interactive fiction. It is also a means of creating new types of reference libraries.[20]

While embracing all of these definitions, Meyrowitz, writing presciently in 1991, saw hypertext as part of a global information infrastructure:

> Down deep, we all think that and believe that hypertext is a vision that sometime soon will be an infrastructure, national and international, that supports a network and community of knowledge linking together myriad types of information for an enormous variety of audiences.[21]

The above quote seems perfectly obvious when writing nearly twenty years after the introduction of the World Wide Web. Linking hypertext to the Internet, however, as early on as Meyrowitz did, was remarkably insightful.[22] As argued at greater length in subsequent chapters of this book, hypertext and hypermedia, particularly as suggested by the work of earlier pioneers such as Vannevar Bush, takes on its greater meaning in the context of augmented cognition and networked information systems.

Augmented Cognition and Intelligence

Computers are increasingly being recognized as providing a means by which to enhance cognition or augment intelligence. The concept of the computer as a "cognition enhancer" means that "the complementary cognitive strengths of a person and a computer can be used in partnership."[23] Computers can, for example, have large, short-term memories. Humans have much more limited short terms memories. Computers can execute complex "algorithms" much more quickly and precisely than humans.[24] In contrast, "people store information over the long term in rich semantic "networks" containing webs of associationally related textual, temporal and visual imagery."[25]

Hypertext and hypermedia systems, as well as simulation and visualization programs, spreadsheets, word processing and graphic design programs, all allow the user to draw on the computer's strengths in "structured symbolic manipulation," while permitting him or her to take advantage of its ability to use semantic networks.

By providing tools that redefine the nature of cognition, the new computer technologies in turn redefine knowledge and thus the nature of literacy and education. Using the computer as a means of enhancing one's cognition—of augmenting one's intelligence—was first analyzed in detail in the early 1960s by Douglas C. Engelbart.

In 1963, Engelbart, who was then working at the Stanford Research Institute, published "A Conceptual Framework for the Augmentation of Man's Intellect."[26] In this essay, he not only outlined the basic principles of word-processing, but also the use of icon systems for computers, as well as technologies such as the computer mouse and scanning.

Engelbart anticipated many of the innovations that have become the foundation of the contemporary computer revolution. At the same time, he outlined many of the key issues involved in the use of the computer—particularly those involving the potential extension of creativity and intelligence through the use of the computer.

What did Engelbart mean when he spoke of "augmenting man's intellect"? According to him:

> By "augmenting man's intellect" we mean increasing the capability of a man to approach a complex problem situation, gain comprehension to suit his particular needs, and to derive solutions to problems. Increased capability in this respect is taken to mean a mixture of the following: that comprehension can be gained more quickly; that better comprehension can be gained more quickly; that better comprehension can be gained; that a useful degree of comprehension can be gained where previously the situation was too complex; that solutions can be produced more quickly; that better solutions can be produced; that solutions can be found where previously the human could find none.[27]

Complex situations, for example, include problems faced by diplomats, executives, social scientists, life scientists, physical scientists, attorneys and designers.[28] Through the use of electronic aids such as computers, Engelbart proposed the emergence of a way of life "in an integrated domain" where "hunches, cut-and-try, intangibles, and the human "feel for a situation" would "coexist with powerful concepts, streamlined terminology and notation, sophisticated methods, and high-powered electronic aids."[29]

Engelbart maintained that the effect which an individual has on the world is essentially dependent on "what he can communicate to it through his limited motor channels."[30] The individual's communication is in turn dependent on what information he has received through his limited sensory channels, his personal needs and how he processes that information. The processing of information is of two kinds: the first of which he is generally conscious and the second at a more unconscious or intuitive level.[31]

The need to address increasingly complex and multi-faceted problems led, according to Engelbart, to the development of *augmentation means*.[32] These include four separate classes:

1. *Artifacts*—physical objects designed to provide for human comfort, the manipulation of things or materials and the manipulation of symbols.
2. *Language*—the way in which the individual classifies the picture

of his world into the concepts that he uses to model that world, and the symbols that he attaches to those concepts and uses in consciously manipulating the concepts ("thinking").

3.   *Methodology*—the methods, procedures, and strategies with which an individual organizes his *goal-centered* (problem-solving) activity.

4.   *Training*—the conditioning needed by the individual to bring his skills in using augmentation means 1, 2, and 3 to the point where they are operationally effective.[33]

Engelbart conceived of a system involving a trained individual using an integrated computer system to manipulate artifacts, employ language and use specific methodologies. Through the use of augmentation means, the individual would be able to break down complex problems into *process hierarchies*. Through their use, the individual (or a group of individuals working together) could "subdivide a large problem in such a way that the human being can walk through it in little steps."[34]

When undertaking a new task an individual draws on a group of sensory-mental capabilities to which he adds the process capabilities of the artifacts that are available to him.[35] In writing this book, for example, the author has drawn on sensory-mental capabilities such as the ability to write, to logically structure arguments, etc., while the word-processor (software, computer and printer) that this document is being created with represent the artifacts that make possible processing capability.

Following Engelbart's construct, the use of a word-processing system to write a book represents a "Human using Language, Artifacts, and Methodology, in which he is Trained" or what he calls a H-LAM/T system.[36] In explaining his H-LAM/T system, Engelbart outlines the basic principles of a word-processor, as well as a scanning system for encoding printed text. The device:

is held like a pencil and, instead of a point, has a special sensing mechanism which can be moved along a line of the special printing from your writing machine (or one like it). The signals which this reading stylus sends through the flexible connecting wire to the writing machine are used to determine which characters are being sensed, thus causing the automatic typing of a duplicate string of characters.[37]

A storage mechanism is included onto which information can be downloaded and stored. Although many aspects of the system Engelbart describes are awkward, it represents an accurate description of many of the essential characteristics of current word-processing and scanning systems that are widely in use today.

What is important from a conceptual view is Engelbart's understanding of the significance of augmentation devices for redefining the process of writing. According to him, the machine/system that he outlines:

> permits you to use a new process of composing text. For instance, trial drafts can rapidly be composed from rearranged excerpts of old drafts, together with new words or passages which you insert by hand typing. Your first draft may represent a free outpouring of thoughts in any order, with the inspection of foregoing thoughts continuously stimulating new considerations and ideas to be entered.[38]

Ideas can be reordered and new ideas can be integrated more easily. More complex procedures can be introduced into the process. According to Engelbart, the important thing to realize is that:

> a direct new innovation in one particular capability can have far-reaching effects throughout the rest of your capability hierarchy. A change can propagate *up* through the capability hierarchy, higher-order capabilities that can utilize the initially changed capability can now reorganize to take special advantage of this change and of the intermediate higher-capability changes. A change can propagate *down* through the hierarchy as a result of new capabilities at the high level and modification possibilities latent in the lower levels.[39]

Engelbart sees the introduction of a writing device of the type he described as having a major impact on how an individual functions at virtually all levels of his or her work and thought.

> Even so apparently minor an advance as artifacts for rapid mechanical duplication and rearrangement of text during the course of creative thought process could yield changes in an individual's repertory hierarchy that would represent a great increase in over-all effectiveness.[40]

Hypertext and hypermedia radically redefine our capacity to manipulate symbols and to control data. Similar results, as we will see, are achieved through the use of simulation software. Following Engelbart's line of thought, such systems have the capability of increasing our capacity to manipulate symbols in ways that have a potentially profound impact on our use of language and our methods of thinking.[41] They become tools embedded in our literacy.[42]

Networked Information Systems: The Internet, the World Wide Web, and Beyond

In *Understanding Media*, first published in 1964, Marshall McLuhan explained how "after more than a century of electronic technology, we have extended our central nervous system itself in a global embrace, abolishing both space and time as far as our planet is concerned."[43] McLuhan was primarily referring to television and radio. His comments, however, resonate even more powerfully in light of the recent emergence of computer-based networked communication systems such as the Internet and the World Wide Web.

Whether under the rubric of the Information Superhighway, Cyberspace, the Internet, the Matrix, or the World Wide Web, a massive worldwide information network is emerging that has the potential to integrate previously separated computer technologies and cultures. Through the Internet, we are seeing the emergence of a linked global information system not unlike the one envisaged by Marshall McLuhan over thirty years ago.

As I will argue in Chapter 4, this new information network incorporates, to varying degrees, the technologies of hypertext and hypermedia. Combined together, they are part of the larger phenomenon that is the "Difference Engine."

The Difference Engine is distinctly post-modern. I believe that in its various forms (fiber optics, satellite transmission of data, cloud and mobile computing, to name just a few) are creating new models of culture, society, art and education. As I argued—drawing heavily on the work of Marshall McLuhan—in my earlier book, *Beyond the Gutenberg Galaxy*, technologies such as television, and in particular the computer, are "bringing to an end typographic culture and creating in its place a post-typographic culture and consciousness."[44]

This consciousness is potentially a "linked" or connected consciousness as part of the Difference Engine and its various elements. Networking, for example, as reflected in the Internet and World Wide Web combining together with Englebart's use of the computer as a cognition enhancer to create a component within the larger Difference Engine—what theorists like Douglas Engelbart and Pierre Levy have referred to as "Collective IQ" or "collective intelligence."[45]

Collective Intelligence

The idea of collective intelligence has been anticipated for years. In 1938, long before the introduction of computers, the science fiction writer H. G. Wells proposed the idea of a "World Brain."[46] Wells's terminology is unfortunate, but the idea extremely interesting.[47] He was convinced that with the passage of time, there would be an encyclopedic and worldwide network of knowledge, one that would be "alive and growing, changing continually . . . every university and research institute feeding it...every fresh mind brought into contact with it . . . its contents the source of the instructional side of school and college work."[48]

Wells's World Brain would not simply be a compilation of facts and data, but instead, a synthesis of the world's knowledge, "an organ of adjustment, adjudication, a clearinghouse of misunderstandings."[49] The World Brain was not practical at the time that he proposed it, since there was no communication system adequate to tie the world's knowledge together. Such a system is now possible because of the existence of the Internet and World Wide Web.[50]

In fact, Douglas Engelbart had envisioned the idea of a linked and collective intelligence or knowledge network as an essential part of his more general work on computing and the augmentation of intelligence. Many of his most famous inventions like synchronous distributed share-screen conferencing, windowing systems, outlining tools, and the mouse were simply devices that would provide "support for the larger goal of augmenting communities of collaborating knowledge workers."[51] For Engelbart, the Internet and World Wide Web simply make this process more feasible

How does this take place? In his essay, "Toward Augmenting the Human Intellect and Boosting our Collective I.Q.," Engelbart explains that he views the computer simply as a tool for supporting Collective IQ. His main means for doing so is through a key integrative paradigm, the "Concurrent Development, Integration and Application of Knowledge" (CoDIAK).[52]

> Key to CoDiak is an open hypertext document system or OHS, which, according to Engelbart, is "an integrated, seamless multi-vendor architecture in which knowledge workers share hyperdocuments on shared screens."[53] Such a hyperdocument system enables the "flexible, on-line collaborative development, integration, application and reuse of CoDiak knowledge."[54]

Engelbart's acronymns and descriptions on decoding, while at times obscure, represent a remarkable vision. Essentially, he argues that through the World Wide Web and even more sophisticated systems it becomes possible to create a networked system of world knowledge:

Every knowledge object—from the largest document, to aggregate branches, down to content units such as characters—has an unambiguous address, understandable and readable by a user, and referenceable anywhere in the hyperdocument system.[55]

Hyperdocuments of the type described by Engelbart are just beginning to be created in large numbers on the Internet and the World Wide Web.[56]

Implicit in the idea of Collective Intelligence is the idea of people joining together and sharing their knowledge, as well as the idea of dialogue and working on problems in conjunction with other people. For Douglas Engelbart this means that groups of scholars, scientists or businessmen have a collective rather than just an individual intelligence. As he explains:

The Collective IQ of a group is a function of how quickly and intelligently it can respond to a situation. This goes well beyond getting more information faster, to include leveraging its collective memory, perception, planning, reasoning, foresight, and experience into applicable knowledge. Such knowledge includes not only the captured knowledge products, such as documentation, plans, and source code, but also the accumulating "web" of issues, lessons learned, rationale, commentary, dialog records, intelligence sources, and so on that iterate throughout the life-cycle of a project or situation.[57]

The development of such systems has profound implications for education. According to Parker Rossman, it is likely that:

the primary importance of mind-empowering computer tools for the electronic university lies not in machines that will think for scholars but scholars using such tools to amplify "collective intelligence," bringing many minds together for more effective collaborative research. The university at its best has been not only a place where specialized individuals work, but has long involved collective intelligence, most often in our time seen in the discourse at professional meetings and through scholarly journals. The global enlargement and empowerment of this process, to make possible a quality of joint work and thought that has never before been realized, is an important aspect of the emerging invisible world of the electronic university.[58]

Collective Intelligence, part of a networked knowledge system imbedded in the Internet and World Wide Web, becomes yet another component or element of the Difference Engine. New types of consiousness are now possible together with even new ways of constructing reality. The most important of these is the concept of hyperreality.

Hyperreality

Hyperreality is a concept developed by the French social theorist Jean Baudrillard. It has been elaborated on by a number of other critics as well and essentially argues that we have entered a world in which media such as television and computers have created a culture of simulation in which the "hyperreal" takes the place of the real.[59] According to Baudrillard, we are in a world where there are:

> No more mirrors of being and appearances, of the real and its concept. No more imaginary coextensity: rather, genetic miniaturization is the dimension of simulation. The real is produced from miniaturized units, from matrices, memory banks and command models—and with these it can be reproduced an infinite number of times. It no longer has to be rational, since it is no longer measured against some ideal or negative instance. It is nothing more than operational. In fact, since it is no longer enveloped by an imaginary, it is no longer real at all. It is hyperreal, the product of an irradiating synthesis of combinatory models in hyperspace without atmosphere.[60]

For Baudrillard, contemporary culture has substituted the map or simulation of things for reality. In his book *Simulations*, for example, he describes how the Argentinean writer Jorge Luis Borges created a tale where the cartographers of an empire drew a map that was so detailed that it covered all of the things it was supposed to represent. When the empire fell into decline, the map rotted away, merging with the soil it had once covered and obscured.[61] What is left is a hyperreality, what Baudrillard describes as:

> the generation by models of a real without origin or a reality: a hyperreal. The territory no longer precedes the map, nor survives it. Henceforth, it is the map that precedes the territory—*precession of simulacra*—it is the map that engenders the territory.[62]

At what point does the simulation act as a map or guide to the reality that we are trying to decode? At what point does it obscure that reality? When does it become the reality? How do we come to distinguish the real from the unreal? These are the ultimate questions raised by Baudrillard about the culture of simulation and the meaning of hyperreality.

As mentioned earlier, there are many discussions of hyperreality beyond those of Baudrillard. The Italian semiotician Umberto Eco talks about holography, Disneyland and reproductions of daVinci's painting "The Last Supper" as being hyperrealties.[63] According to Douglas Kellner, a hyperreal society of simulations also includes interstate highways, urban freeways, fashion, media, architecture and housing developments and shopping malls.[64] In the context of this work, hyperreality is limited to those simulations constructed through the computer and its associated technologies.

The Panoptic Sort

Rooted in a much more concrete and immediate world than hyperreality is the panoptic sort. Computers, particularly when linked in networks, have an enormous potential to track our every purchase, telephone call, or action. This surveillance is made possible by the computer and its increasingly widespread use. According to David Lyon:

> Most surveillance occurs literally out of sight, in the realm of digital signals. And it happen . . . not in clandestine, conspiratorial fashion, but in the commonplace transactions of shopping, voting, phoning, driving and working. This means that people seldom know that they are subjects of surveillance, or, if they do know, they are unaware how comprehensive others knowledge of them actually is.[65]

Most of us need only request a copy of our credit history from a computerized finacial service or take a look at a supermarket receipt to realize the extent to which we are under continuous surveillance.The idea of surveillance as a means of control is not new. In the eighteenth century, the English utilitarian philosopher Jeremy Bentham proposed a system of social control or *panopticonism*, which kept the individual, whether a prisoner, hospital inmate or student, under continual surveillance. Michel Foucault, in *Discipline and Punish*, argues that Bentham's work represented the recognition of a new type of power and control being introduced in Western society—one in which information about people and their actions are constantly tracked and sorted.[66]

This process of what Foucault refers to as *normalization* has come to be realized in our own era through instrumentalities provided initially by mainframe computers and in turn by microcomputers. Referred to as the *panoptic sort*, the individual is kept under control by his or her having a continuous stream of data collected about them. With this information the individual can be regulated and controlled.

As I will argue in Chapter 6, I believe that the panoptic sort—so suggestive of George Orwell's dystopian vision of Big Brother in his novel *1984*—is both frightening and dehumanizing. It is also a technology largely made possible through the technology of the computer—specifically networked systems and the Internet. When combined with the culture of simulation, and more specifically, with hyperreality, we are faced with a profound social challenge—one which threatens many of our basic rights and democratic principles.

Mobile Computing

Mobile computing refers to the idea of using a computing device while in transit. Initially, mobile computing was synonymous with portable computing. The first portable computer was patented in 1979 by James D. Murez for GM Research in Carson City. California.[67] It was followed shortly afterward by the Osborne 1 computer. Apple Incorporated introduced a portable machine in 1984. These early devices were "luggable" machines. These machines and their successors could not easily be used in transit. Mobile machines have come into use largely in the first decade of the Twenty-First Century. Often these devices are not identified as computers, but take the form of cell phones, digital assistants, small notebooks and tablet computers. It is clear that these devices are revolutionizing current computing and that they can be looked at collectively as the most recent iteration of the Difference Engine.

Mobile computing is particularly important, because it brings computing into almost every aspect of our lives. People are constantly available via their cell phones. Messages can be sent from a personal digital assistant at anytime in almost any place. The Internet and World Wide Web can easily be accessed from a phone, a digital assistant or tablet computer. Electronic books suddenly have the potential to truly redefine the experience of reading, as they bring interactive screen, sound, and motion picture and animations to what had previously been the static printed page. A new type of literacy suddenly becomes possible—one that will continue to evolve and develop in years to come.

*   *   *

The seven technologies of *Hypertext/Hypermedia, Augmented Cognition and Intelligence, Networked Information and Communication Systems, Collective Intelligence, Hyperreality,* the *Panoptic Sort* and *Mobile Computing* overlap and combine together to create the Difference Engine. While important on their own, it is in their combined function that they take on their true significance and meaning. They are part of post-typographic and post-modern culture and need to be understood as part of a profound cultural and social transformation that is already underway.

Post-Typographic and Post-Modernism

The idea of the emergence of a post-typographic culture, which McLuhan so clearly anticipated, was recognized by other theorists as well. The most important of these is the cultural theorist Jean-Francois Lyotard. In his 1979 work *La Condition Postmoderne: Rapport Sur le Savoir,* Lyotard argued that Western culture has entered a post-modern period in which traditional narratives of science and culture have been redefined.[68] Describing knowledge in computerized societies, Lyotard argued that the status of knowledge was altered when we entered the post-modern age. This process probably began some time in the 1950s with the completion of Europe's reconstruction following the Second World War and continues into our own era.[69]

At its most basic level, Lyotard describes post-modernism "as incredulity towards metanarratives."[70] Traditional models of knowledge, communication and learning have been transformed as a result of new forms of media, information transfer and cybernetics or computers.[71] As this has occurred, the present has become a confusing and alien territory for most people—a frontier whose meaning is unfolding around them. As Marshall McLuhan explained in the early 1960s:

> We are today as far into the electric age as the Elizabethans had advanced into the typographical and mechanical age. And we are experiencing the same confusions and indecisions which they had felt when living in two contrasted forms of society and experience. Whereas the Elizabethans were poised between medieval corporate experience and modern individualism, we reverse their pattern by confronting an electric technology which would seem to render individualism obsolete and the corporate interdependence mandatory.[72]

McLuhan implicitly argued that we had crossed a cultural divide between what Lyotard argues is a post-modern culture and the older typographic culture. In other words, we have left the Gutenberg Galaxy that has dominated our consciousness and interpretation of our culture for the past five hundred years and have entered into a new post-typographic or post-modern culture.

By extending the means by which we communicate—first through writing, then through printing as part of the typographic era, and now through radio, television and computers (including derivative technologies such as cellphones), we are ironically returning to traditions more typically associated with the tribalism of oral cultures. Through these new media we are more interactive in our communication process than was the case in the more closed and narrowly defined traditions of typographic culture. As McLuhan explains:

> Now, in the electric age, the very instantaneous nature of co-existence among our technological instruments has created a crisis quite unique in human history. Our extended faculties and senses now constitute a single field of experience which demands that they become collectively conscious.[73]

If what McLuhan argues is true, then the character and nature of culture can never be the same. Computerization, and more specifically the Difference Engine, is at the center of, and drives, this process of cultural transformation.

Post-Modernism and the New Pluralism

McLuhan argued that any culture that is moving from one modality of consciousness, from the oral to the visual, for example, is unavoidably caught in a process of artistic change and ferment. We are undergoing just such a process in contemporary culture, as we redefine the meaning of literacy through out use of computers as part of the Analytic Engine. Images or metaphors that were accepted and taken for granted as common knowledge are now subject to challenge. The nature of research and knowledge, the function of language, the meaning of music and art, the role of women in our culture, the meaning of race or nationality, definitions of beautiful and truth are subject to radical redefinition. According to McLuhan, "we become extremely conscious of cultural models and bias when moving from one dominant form of awareness to another."[74]

In *The Global Village* McLuhan and Bruce R. Powers discuss "robotism" or "right-hemisphere thinking." This represents the "capacity to be a conscious presence in many places at once."[75] McLuhan and Powers argue that the interactive nature of selected video-related technologies will produce robotism or what I prefer to describe as a post-modern pluralism. According to McLuhan and Powers:

> The United States by 2020 will achieve a distinct psychological shift from a dependence on visual, uniform, homogeneous thinking, of a left-hemisphere variety, to a multi-faceted configurational mentality which we have attempted to define as audile-tactile, right-hemisphere thinking. In other words, instead of being captured by point-to-point linear attitudes, so helpful to the mathematician and the accountant, most Americans will

be able to tolerate many different thought systems at once, some based on antagonistic ethnic heritages.[76]

The value placed on precise scientific and quantitative ordering will almost certainly give way to more qualitative and metaphorical ways of knowing.[77] I believe that many models will compete and be accepted in the new culture. The possibilities of choice and difference will be facilitated by the new media and its accompanying computer technologies. This shift represents what I refer to as "digital rhetoric." As a phenomenon it is distinctly postmodern and is a result of the existence of the Difference Engine.

On the Non-Neutrality of the Computer

In the chapters that follow, I have attempted to frame my arguments in ways that resonate with the questions and issues raised by critical theory. For example, in the context of the work of Jürgen Habermas and his theory of communicative action, I ask in the Conclusion of this work how the different manifestations of the "Difference Engine" contribute to what he terms "the ideal speech situation." In doing so, I wish to address the larger question of how computers function to empower those who use them, or how they instead can alienate and be used to control individuals through what Michel Foucault describes as the power of "Normalization" and what I and other theorists have described as the "electronic panopticon."[78] In following this line of thought, I am consciously challenging those technophiles and educational technologists—and educators in general—whom I believe have little understanding of the fact that while computers are, on one level, only machines, that they are also socially constructed and value-laden.

In this context, it must be understood that computers and the programs that run on them are neither neutral, nor without consequences. In turn, neither hypertext and hypermedia, simulation technology, the panoptic sort nor the Internet are neutral. While in certain regards all have the potential to expand our creativity, imagination and understanding of the world, they also can limit our freedom and what it means to be human.[79]

C. A. Bowers, in his important work *The Cultural Dimensions of Educational Computing*, questions, in reference to educational computing, whether or not the computer is a neutral technology. According to him:

> the most fundamental question about the new technology has never been seriously raised by either the vocal advocates or the teachers who have attempted to articulate their reservations. The question has to do with whether the technology is neutral; that is, neutral in terms of accurately

representing, at the level of the software program, the domains of the real world in which people live.[80]

Bowers argues that computers and their software must be understood as "part of the much more complex symbolic world that makes up our culture."[81] According to Bowers, we need to critically reframe how we look at computers and how they function. Instead of simply understanding them in a technical and procedural context, we need to deal with them in a larger cultural context—how they mediate and change our systems of knowledge and ways of interpreting the world around us.[82] In doing so, we must ask what it is that *Hypertext/Hypermedia, Augmented Cognition and Intelligence, Networked Information and Communication Systems, Collective Intelligence, Hyperreality,* and the *Panoptic Sort* select for *amplification* and for *reduction*?[83] We must also ask how they interact and combine with each other—i.e., as part of the Difference Engine. My attempts to answer this question structure my discussion in the chapters that follow.

Notes

1.   Theodor Holm Nelson, *Literary Machines, Edition 87.1* (The Report On, And Of, Project Xanadu Concerning Word Processing, Electronic Publishing, Hypertext, Thinkertoys, Tomorrow's Intellectual Revolution, And Certain Other Topics Including Knowledge, Education And Freedom) (Bellevue, WA: Microsoft Press, 1987), p. 1/5.

2.   Vannevar Bush, "As We May Think," *Atlantic Monthly*, July 1945, pp. 101-108. This article is reprinted in part in Nelson's *Literary Machines*, pp. 1/39-1/54. A full reprint of the article can be found in Irene Greif, ed., *Computer-Supported Cooperative Work: A Book of Readings* (San Fracisco, CA: Morgan Kaufmann Publishers, Inc., 1988), pp. 17-34. *Ibid*, p. 30.

3.   *Ibid*. For background on Bush and the Memex and its relationship to hypertext see: *From Memex to Hypertext: Vannevar Bush and the Mind's Machine*, edited by James M. Nyce and Paul Kahn (Boston: Academic Press, 1991).

4.   *Ibid*.

5.   *Ibid.*, p. 30.

6.   *Ibid*.

7.   *Ibid.*, p. 31.

8.   *Ibid*.

9.   *Ibid.*, pp. 31-32.

10. *Ibid*.

11. *Ibid.*, p. 32.

12. *Ibid.*, p. 34.

13. *Ibid.*, p. 0/2.

14. *Ibid*.

15. George P. Landow, "The Rhetoric of Hypermedia: Some Rules for Authors," *Journal of Computing in Higher Education*, vol. 1, no. 1 (Spring 1989), p. 39.

16. Jeff Conklin, "Hypertext: An Introduction and Survey," *Computer*, vol. 20, no. 9, p. 17.

17. Michael Joyce, *Of Two Minds: Hypertext Pedagogy and Politics* (Ann Arbor: University of Michigan Press, 1995), p. 19.

18. *Ibid.*, pp. 23-24.

19. *Ibid.*, p. 24.

20. Norman Meyrowitz, "Hypertext—Does It Reduce Cholesterol, Too?" included in James Nyce and Paul Kahn editors, *From Memex to Hyperttext: Vannevar Bush and the Mind's Machine* (Boston: Academic Press, Inc., 1991), pp. 287-288.

21. *Ibid.*, p. 288.

22. The stunning expansion of the Google search engine into a comprehensive academic search system makes clear the emerging reality of the Internet and World Wide Web as a demonstration of the global network rapidly coming into place that is described by Meyerwitz. To better understand the implications of Google and Google Scholar for the creation of a networked global information infrastructure see: "About Google Scholar" (http://scholar.google.com/scholar/about.html).

23. Christopher J. Dede, "Empowering Environments, Hypermedia and Microworlds, *The Computing Teacher*, November 1987, p. 21.

24. *Ibid.*

25. *Ibid.*

26. Douglas Engelbart, "A Conceptual Framework for the Augmentation of Man's Intellect," P. W. Howerton and D. C. Weeks, *Vistas in Information Handling: Vol. 1. The Augmentation of Man's Intellect by Machine* (Washington, DC: Spartan Books, 1963), pp. 1-29.

27. *Ibid.*, p. 1.

28. *Ibid.*

29. *Ibid.*

30. *Ibid.*, p. 3.

31. *Ibid.*

32. As Engelbart explained: "Man's population and gross product are increasing at a considerable rate, but the complexity of his problems grows even faster. And the urgency with which solutions must be found becomes steadily greater in response to the increased rate of activity and the increasingly global nature of the activity." *Ibid*, p. 4.

33. *Ibid.*

34. *Ibid.*

35. *Ibid.*, p. 5.

36. *Ibid.*

37. *Ibid.*, p. 7.

38. *Ibid.*, p. 7.

39. *Ibid.*, p. 7.

40. *Ibid.*, p. 9.

41. *Ibid.*, p. 15.

42. An obvious example of how this has occurred is the invention during the late 1970s of microcomputer spreadsheet systems such as VisiCalc. Prior to computer spreadsheets: "If one monthly expense went up or down, everything—*everything*—had to be recalculated. It was a tedious task, and few people who earned their MBAs at Harvard expected to work with spreadsheets very much. Making spreadsheets, however necessary, was a dull chore best left to accountants, junior analysts, or secretaries. As for sophisticated "modeling" tasks—which, among other things, enable executives to project costs for their companies—these tasks could be done only on big mainframe computers by the data-processing people who worked for the companies Harvard MBAs managed." (Steven Levy, "People and Computers in Commerce: A Spreadsheet Way of Knowledge," in Tom Forester, ed., *Computers in the Human Context* (Massachusetts: MIT Press, 1989), p. 319.)

Dan Bricklin, the inventor of VisiCalc, came up with the idea for computer spreadsheets while sitting in a business class at Harvard and wanting to avoid the drudgery of constantly recalculating ledger sheets.

43. Marshall McLuhan, *Understanding Media: The Extensions of Man* (New York: Mentor Books, 1964), p. 19.

44. Eugene F. Provenzo, Jr., *Beyond the Gutenberg Galaxy: Microcomputers and the Emergence of Post-Typographic Culture* (New York: Teachers College Press, 1986),

pp. 3-4.

45. See the references to Englebart and his work in the previous chapter and also visit his Bootstrap Institute at: http://www.bootstrap.org/ which includes extensive documentation about his efforts to create a system of shared or collective intelligence, or what Engelbart refers to as "Collective IQ." A particularly valuable overview is provided in the web slide site "Boosting Collective I. Q." found at the address: http://www.bootstrap.org/vision.htm.

46. H. G. Wells, *World Brain* (Garden City, NJ: Doubleday Doran, 1938).

47. Parker Rossman, *The Emerging Worldwide Electronic University: Information Age Global Higher Education* (Westport, CN: Prager, 1993), p. 73.

48. Quoted by *Rossman*, p. 73.

49. *Ibid*, p. 74.

50. As mentioned earlier, Google in its efforts to create a meta search engine for scholars in the form of Google Scholar, as well as a functioning world library, represent some of the first clear steps forward in making such a dream come true. Google is currently working with the Library of Congress and leading academic libraries such as Stanford University, Harvard University, University of Michigan, Oxford University and the New York Public Library to scan and make available in a global electronic library materials no longer in copyright or for which the copyright has been waived. See: David A. Vise, "World Digital Library Planned Library of Congress Envisions Collection to Bridge Cultures," *Washington Post*, November 22, 2005, p. A27.

51. Douglas Englebart, "Augment, Bootstrap Communities, the Web: What Next?" Available at: www.bootstrap.org/chi98demo.htm

52. Douglas Engelbart, "Toward Augmenting the Human Intellect and Boosting our Collective I. Q.," *Communications of the ACM*, Vol. 38, 8, August 1995, p. 30.

53. *Ibid*.

54. *Ibid*.

55. *Ibid*, p. 32.

56. Among the most important of these is the site for the Human Genome Project (www.ornl.gov/sci/techresources/Human_Genome/home.shtml), that had as its purpose identifying all of the approximately 20,000-25,000 genes in human DNA, determining the sequences of the 3 billion chemical base pairs that make up human DNA, and storing this information in databases. In the Humanities, several superb pioneering hypertext sites have been developed by the English scholar, art historian and hypertext theorist, George Landow, a professor at Brown University. Many of George Landow's sites, which include the Victorian Web, were originally developed as CD-ROM hypermedia systems. With the widespread introduction and use of the World Wide Web he moved them onto the Internet. These remarkable web systems represent the first online stages of Engelbart's vision of Collective IQ systems. They hearken back to Vannevar Bush's 1945 essay "As We May Think," Vannevar argued that in the not too distant future new types of encyclopedia would be created as part of his "Memex" system that would have a: "mesh of associative trails running through them, ready to be dropped into the Memex and there amplified. The lawyer has at his fingertips the associated opinions and decisions of his whole experience and

of the experience of friends and authorities. The patent attorney has on call the millions of issued patents, with familiar trails to every point of his client's interest. The physician puzzled by a patient's reaction strikes the trail established in studying an earlier similar case, and runs rapidly through analogous case histories, with side references to the classics for the pertinent anatomy and histology. . . . The historian, with a vast chronological account of a people parallels it with a skip trail which stops only on the salient items, and can follow at any time contemporary trails which lead him all over civilization at a particular epoch."

Bush's description is now a reality, and can be seen at work in pioneering systems such as Brown University's George Landow's Victorian Web (www.stg.brown.edu/projects/hypertext/landow/victorian/victov.html), a project begun by him in the Spring of 1985 as an experiment under the sponsorhip of Brown University's Institute for Research in Information and Scholarship (IRIS), has expanded over the years to include a wide-range of students and scholars. While Landow designed and edited the original site and was responsible for most of the original materials, others began to contribute to the system as well. After describing his own contribution to the creation of the site, Landow explains how different scholars and students began contributing to the system. In 1994, for example, students in Landow's Victorian literature course created more than a hundred new documents or "lexias" for the web. After Landow edited them, they were added to the online system. At his web site, Landow lists some of the most recent additions by students and others to the project and its content (www.stg.brown.edu/projects/hypertext/landow/victorian/misc/1995contrib.html).

In the case of the text for *Alice in Wonderland* and *Through the Looking Glass,* an extensive series of student commentaries on specialized topics are included online. These include: Serra Ansay '96, "Inventions in Alice in Wonderland," Rachel Hannah Beck '96, "Lunacy in the Ballroom: A Carollian Take on Traditional Mores," Joshua Bloustine '98, "Capitalism in Through the Looking Glass," Robert Chapman '98, "Pig and Pepper and Social Theory," Kate Egan '97, "Money in the Alice Books," Katie Krauskopf '97, "Alice and the Victorian Gentleman, Game of Words: The Ambiguities of Language in Great Expectations and Through the Looking-Glass," Elizabeth Lee '97, "The White Knight and the Victorian Gentleman," May Lee '97, "Alice–Mutton: Mutton–Alice: Parodies of Protocol in Through the Looking Glass," Sarah Polisner '98, "Victorian Growth and Self-Discovery in Alice's Adventures in Wonderland," Dan Ratner '97, "Victorian Hunger and Malnutrition in Alice in Wonderland," Anya Weber '96.5, "Food, Drink, and Public Health in the Alice Books," and Susan W. Wong '96, "Class in the Garden of Live Flowers."

With his Victorian Web Landow is doing something revolutionary as both a teacher and as a researcher. To begin with, he is breaking down the walls between students and scholarly research. Acting as a guide and editor, Landow's student projects find a place for publication that is open to a worldwide audience. In addition, he creates a space where scholars other than himself can contribute their unique perspective and knowledge. (There is an open invitation on the site for any scholar to contact Landow and contribute materials to his system.)

Landow is creating a hypermedia/web environment in which collective knowledge can be drawn together, organized and extended. His Victorian Web is by no means limited to just his own intelligence and knowledge, or even to that of the people he has provided a publishing space for, but is also linked to other web sites with information relevant to his topic. Thus, Landow connects from his page in the Victorian Web devoted to "The Arts in Victorian Britain" (ww.stg.brown.edu/projects/hypertext/landow/victorian/art/artov.html) site to Russell A. Potter's online review of the book *The Panorama: History of a Mass Medium* included in the electronic journal *Iconomania: Studies in Visual Culture* (www.humnet.ucla.edu/Icono/rapotter/panoram.htm). Landow's work for The Victorian Web is much more than just an interesting research project. It redefines the process of scholarly publishing. Students' work and the work of different colleagues around the world are reviewed by Landow and judged as being good enough to include on his system. A system like his has a huge audience with thousands of visitors a year. Is inclusion on his web, which has a huge user base, equivalent to a juried publication?

57. Douglas Engelbart, "Boosting Collective IQ." Available at the Englebart's web site: www.bootstrap.org/vision.htm.

58. Rossman, p. 58

59. See, for example: William Bogard, "Sociology in the Absence of the Social: The Significance of Baudrillard for Contemporary Thought," *Philosophy and Social Criticism*, 13, No. 3, 1987, pp. 227-242; Douglas Kellner, *Jean Baudrillard: From Marxism to Postmodernism and Beyond* (Stanford, CA: Stanford University Press, 1989); and Timothy W. Luke, "Touring Hyperreality: Critical Theory Confronts Informational Society," in Philip Wexler, editor, *Critical Theory Now* (London: Falmer Press, 1991), pp. 1-26.

60. Jean Baudrillard, *Simulations*, translated by Paul Foos, Paul Patton and Philip Beitchman (New York: Semiotext(e), 1983), p. 3.

61. *Ibid.*, p. 1.

62. *Ibid.*, p. 2.

63. Eco, Umberto, *Travels in Hyperreality*, translated by William Weaver (New York: Harcourt Brace & Company, 1990).

64. *Kellner*, p. 83. According to Kellner, "In a hyperreal world the model comes first, and its constitutive role is invisible, because all one sees are instatiations of models (while one reproduces models of thought and behavior oneself)."

65. David Lyon, *The Electronic Eye: The Rise of the Surveillance Society* (Minneapolis: University of Minnesota Press, 1994), p. 5. For current resources on electronic surveillance see the resource page of the Electronic Frontier Foundation at: www.eff.org/Privacy/Surveillance/

66. Michel Foucault, *Discipline and Punish*, translated by Alan Sheridan (New York: Random House, 1979).

67. United States Patent, 4,294,496 for a Portable Computer Enclosure, awarded to James D. Murez, October 13, 1981, filed August 3, 1979.

68. Jean-Francois Lyotard, *La Condition Postmoderne: Rapport Sur le Savoir* (Paris: Les Editions de Minuit, 1979).

69. Jean-Francois Lyotard, "Answering the Question: What is Postmodernism?",

included in Charles Jencks, editor, *The Post-Modern Reader* (New York: St. Martin's Press, 1992), p. 138.

70. *Ibid.*, p. 138.

71. *Ibid.*, pp. 139-140.

72. Marshall, McLuhan, *The Gutenberg Galaxy: The Making of Typographic Man* (Toronto: University of Toronto Press, 1962), p. 1.

73. *Ibid*, p. 5.

74. *Ibid*, p. 73.

75. Marshall McLuhan and Bruce R. Powers, *The Global Village: Transformations in World Life and Media in the 21st Century* (Oxford: Oxford University Press, 1989), p. 83.

76. *Ibid*, p. 86.

77. *Ibid*.

78. See Eugene F. Provenzo Jr., "The Electronic Panopticon: Censorship, Control and Indoctrination in a Post-Typographic Culture," in Myron Tuman, editor, *Literacy Online: The Promise (and Peril) of Reading and Writing with Computers* (Pittsburgh: University of Pittsburgh Press, 1992), pp. 167-178. An updated version of this chapter is included as Chapter 7 of this book.

79. In my earlier work *Beyond the Gutenberg Galaxy: Microcomputers and Post-Typographc Culture* (New York: Teachers College Press Press, 1985), I made reference to the work of Ernest Becker and the image of humanity as either machine (*l'homme machine*) or as meaning seekers and meaning makers (*homo poeta*). Like Becker, I argued that we create evil when we design structures or institutions that make it impossible for us to act productively and creatively. Computers in the form of simulations and hypermedia systems have the potential to greatly expand our creativity and imagination and our understanding of the world. However, these systems, based as they are on computers, are not neutral and must be understood in terms of their capacity to shape and direct us. See: Ernest Becker, *The Structure of Evil* (New York: Free Press, 1978), pp. 169-74.

80. C. A. Bowers, *The Cultural Dimensions of Educational Computing: Understanding the Non-Neutrality of Technology* (New York: Teachers College Press, 1980), p. 24.

81. *Ibid*.

82. *Ibid.*, p. 27.

83. *Ibid.*, pp. 32-33.

Chapter 2

Reinventing the Text

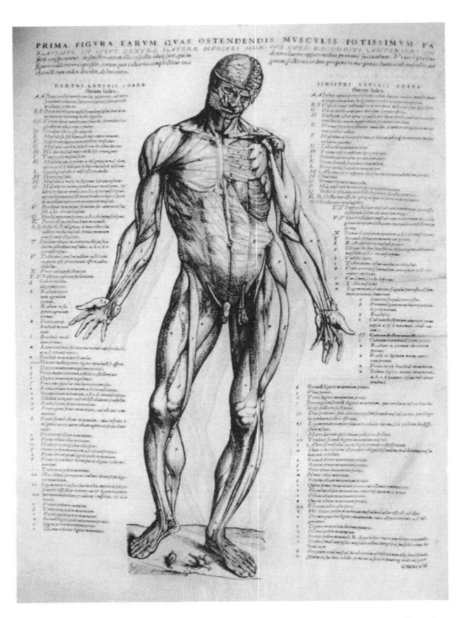

Page from *De Humani coporis fabrica*, printed by Johann Oporinus, 1543, showing the use of Italics and new models of scientific drawing.

A s a teenager not yet in college, I remember sitting in my bedroom in the basement of my parents' home. It was a large room that ran the length of the house. Across one entire wall was a row of bookshelves. I had already begun to develop an unusual fondness for books and already owned fourteen or fifteen hundred volumes.

Included among the books sitting on the shelves were most of the important novelists, poets and historians who were part of the Western literary and historical tradition. There were the Greeks: Homer, Aeschylus, Aristophanes, and of course, Aristotle and Plato. There were Medieval and Renaissance authors: St. Thomas Aquinas, Machiavelli, Guiccardini and Michelangelo. The nineteenth century had its representatives, including: Dickinson, Hardy, Melville, and Whitman.

Looking back, I can recall an intense desire to organize and master the content of these works. I knew instinctively that these books were part of a dialogue, a sacred conversation that extended across Western history. It was certainly not the only dialogue of its type. There were other cultures whose literature and history I was vaguely and largely unaware of.

I knew that in unexpected and significant ways these books were somehow connected—somehow linked across time, different cultures and geographical settings. I remember, for example, having read that Thomas Jefferson had been influenced by authors such as Locke and Machiavelli, but the question for me was how? Answering these questions seemed to be the main object and purpose of my education. The problem was where to begin? What were the links? Where were the connections? I had embarked on a voyage of self-education.

For the experienced scholar in his or her area of specialty, the connections and links, ultimately the meaning of a subject, is different than for a beginner in the field. Literacy is not the same for each individual, but instead is defined by the cumulative experience and knowledge of the reader. George Landow makes this point in describing a Milton scholar sitting down with her copy of *Paradise Lost*:

> It is eight pm, and after having helped put the children to bed, Professor Jones settles into her favorite chair and reaches for her copy of Milton's *Paradise Lost* in order to prepare for tomorrow's class. A scholar who specializes in the poetry of Milton's time, she returns to the poem as one returns to meet an old friend. Reading the poem's opening pages, she once again encounters allusions to the Old Testament, and because she knows how seventeenth-century Christians commonly reread these passages, she perceives connections both to a passage in Genesis and to its radical Christian transformations. Furthermore, her previous acquaintance with Milton allows her to recall other passages later in *Paradise Lost* that refer to this and related parts of the Bible. At the same time, she recognizes that the poem's opening lines pay homage to Homer, Virgil, Dante and Spenser and simultaneously issues them a challenge.[1]

Landow goes on to describe how John H. Smith, one of Professor's Jones's most thorough students, is also preparing for class. His reading is far less connected. Most of the allusions found in the poem go unrecognized by him. Even with the help of footnotes and a dictionary, his reading is limited and circumscribed compared to that of Professor Jones.[2]

This need not be the case. According to Landow, using a hypertext or hypermedia system, Smith:

> ... could touch the opening lines of *Paradise Lost,* for instance, and the relevant passage from Homer, Virgil, and the Bible would appear, or that he could touch another line and immediately receive a choice of other mentions of the same idea or image in the poem or elsewhere in Milton's other writings—or, for that matter, interpretations and critical judgements made since the poem's first publication.[3]

Had such a system been available to me as a teenager, my problem of how to begin to discover the connections and links found in the Western literary and historical tradition would have been much easier. Like Professor Jones's student Smith, I would have been able to track links and connections back to earlier works and to understand the significance of specific references and allusions. In essence, I would have had available to me in a useable form that could be entered on many different levels the contextual and historical variables that define a literary or historical work.

Critically linking texts to other primary sources, as well as to various theoretical and historical literatures, is by no means a new phenomenon. When a scholar writes a footnote he or she is essentially establishing a link to another body of literature. In my own work as a scholar, for example, I have typically employed footnotes not only as a means of crediting my sources, but in order to establish a discussion at a secondary level—one that functions beneath the main current of the text. In a certain sense, a footnote can be seen as a type of primitive hypertext.

Footnote = Link = Primitive Hypertext

The problem with footnotes of course is that the sources they refer to are rarely immediately accessible. You are sitting in your study reading a useful source, but the library is closed, or the book is checked out and so on. If a source is important enough, you eventually track it down. Often the result is that the work cited was not that informative or useful—often not worth the wait or delay it caused in developing a line of inquiry or thought. The beauty of a well-developed hypertext system is that the sources are instantly available in a useable format to the reader. In addition, the reader can, depending on his or her interest and sophistication, delve into the text at different levels of interpretation and complexity. Thus Landow's Professor Jones would employ the hypertext system at one level, going much deeper into links and associative connections, while her student John Smith would delve into the material at another, but for him, appropriate, level.

How important are these connections or links to the reader? To what extent do they play a part in defining what is a literate and "connected" reading of a text? Consider the following Aesopic fable:

On one level the fable can be read as simply a charming story. A hypertext system might provide links connecting this nineteenth-century version of the text back to earlier editions of the fable—possibly going back to its very earliest versions in ancient Greece and Rome. Suppose, however, that you wanted to make the reader aware of the political significance of the fable. A designated button on a hypertext or hypermedia command screen (mouse or touch screen activated) could include a series of screens or files on the political meaning of the fable. The system could be programmed to have key words highlighted that, when activated with a mouse, call up additional information.

Thus by touching the phrase "unity is strength," the image of a dollar bill could be called up on the screen together with a discussion of the importance of the meaning of the motto and why it is used to represent democratic ideals and values.[4] A second highlighted set of words might be "a faggot of sticks." On touching the phrase, a detailed explanation would be presented of the term fascist. *Fascio* is the Latin word for a bundle. The reference to a bundle as part of the Classical Republican tradition in Rome is to the *Fasces*, a bundle of sticks that were banded together and carried on the ends of poles or standards by the Roman legions to signify the unity of the Roman Republic. In Italy and Germany political leaders such as Mussolini and Hitler reinvented the symbol. Besides using the term *fascist*, for example, the Nazi Party combined the symbol of a bundle of sticks with the swastika and carried it on standards much like their Roman predecessors. Illustrations of this can be seen in photographs from the 1932 Nuremberg Rallies. Visual references are also included of Roman legionnaires carrying *Fasces*. References to pertinent articles, as well as a detailed etymological explanation of the term fascist from a source such as the *Oxford English Dictionary* might be included as well. The role of the fable "In Unity is Strength" in defining the evolution of the term *fascist* can be explored in detail.

Finally, the hypertext system might lead its user to other political references involving the interpretation and use of the fable. A link could be made to a file that described how Aesop was among the authors read by Abraham Lincoln, and how he used the fable of "The Old Man and the Bundle of Sticks" ("In Unity is Strength") at various points in his political career.

The system could have a list of all the editions of Aesop published since antiquity that included the fable of "The Old Man and the Bundle of Sticks".

In a large and sophisticated hypertext system, the full texts of these fables could be included as well. Different editions of the fable could be included for comparative purposes. Illustrations of the fable across different time periods and editions could be linked. Annotations showing the connections between different editions could be shown. Commentary about different versions of the fable by major scholars could be provided, and so on.

In this context, hypertext and hypermedia have the potential to liberate the text and the references and connections imbedded within them. In doing so, hypertext and hypermedia can open and reveal—literally liberate the text and the physical constraints by which it is bound, read and interpreted. As will be explored later in this work, it also has the potential to severely limit our access to information and the sources through which we learn.

In Unity Is Strength: The Bundle of Sticks

An old man on the point of death summoned his sons round him to give them some parting advice. He ordered his servants to bring in a faggot of sticks and said to his eldest son: "Break it" The son strained and strained, but with all his efforts was unable to break the Bundle. The other sons also tried, but none of them was successful. "Untie the faggots," said the father, "and each of you take a stick." When he had done so, he called out to them: "Now break," and each stick was easily broken. "You see my meaning," said their father.

"A Union gives strength."

The source of this text is: Joseph Jacobs, *The Fables of Aesop*, illustrated by Richard Heighway, first published in 1894, p. 174.

Fasces, which can be seen behind the figure of the hands and the Constitution, were a faggot of sticks or wooden rods that were fastened around an axe and held together with a leather strap. Fasces were a symbol of the authority and power of the Roman republic and were carried by Roman judges as a symbol of authority. Their origin can be traced back to the fable of "The Old Man and the Bundle of Sticks". Fasces provide the origin for the modern term fascist. Fasces were often incorporated into Nazi propaganda and symbols.

Sequential Versus Non-Sequential Texts

The structure of the book, and its predecessor, the ancient and medieval scroll, is essentially linear in nature. It creates a discourse and progression through a physical text. In general, ideas are not structured or coded in relationship to one another, but presented in the form of a continuous sequential or linear code. Point A leads to Point B and so forth. Thus, in the Book of Genesis there is a sequence and structured discourse that describes how:

> In the beginning God created the heavens and the earth. The earth was without form and void, and darkness was upon the face of the deep; and the Spirit of God was moving over the face of the waters. And God said, "Let there be light"; and there was light.[5]

The text does not have coherent meaning outside of its antecedents. This does not need to be the case with hypertext. Instead, as George Landow argues, hypertext changes the way texts exist and in turn the way we read them. According to him: "The defining characteristics of this new information medium derive from its combination of blocks of text joined by electronic links, for this combination emphasizes multiple connections rather than linear reading or linear organization."[6]

Edward Barrett makes much the same distinction. As he explains:

> The traditional book is read from beginning to the end, so the author can write each page knowing that the reader has just finished the previous page. Electronic documentation, however, is not read as much as referred to. The readers can skip around, and usually just look up one item and then another. Often the documentation for a program is available on paper as well as online.[7]

It should be understood that hypertext in any of its forms is not a totally open system. As will be explored in more detail in subsequent chapters of this work, any hypertext database is structured by the initial programming decisions that are used to establish the program or system. The importance of this lies in the fact that:

> If the internal structure is too highly constrained by the initial programming input, the user is relegated to the position of merely manipulating text-objects through an *a priori* associative web. A collage of conceptual or factual blocks may be achieved, but a deeper structuring of imaginative insights may not be possible.[8]

While hypertext can include sequential or linear forms of writing, it also includes nonlinear structures. Drawing an analogy from science fiction, sequential or linear forms of writing represent a spaceship that follows a particular trajectory through space. In contrast, a hypertext system is like a spacecraft that can follow the trajectory of a rocket, or can make leaps through "hyperspace" that supersede the physics and limitations of a sequential or linear universe.

In a hypertext system, virtually all segments of the text universe can be connected through "links." For practical purposes these links are instantaneous. All that is necessary is that a pathway be defined between the various points in the universe. Drawing again on an analogy from science fiction, using a matter transfer system individuals can be "beamed up" or "down" to virtually any point in the universe. Rather than having to travel in a linear fashion between one point and another, their corporeal selves can be dematerialized (digitized) and transferred to a specific point in space. In much the same way, in a hypertext system the computer can locate specific coordinates and transport a block of text, a photograph, a spreadsheet or a graphic image to a particular subsystem of data within the computer's universe.[9]

Models of satellites rotating around planetary systems, planets that rotate around suns, independent galaxies—radically different and related structures—are just a few of the images that come to mind. A galactic system can be likened to a computer system. Data files can represent planets and moons, which are contained within stellar systems. At a stellar level, the model of an orrery—the mechanical device for representing the motions and phases of the planets and satellites in the solar system—comes to mind. Each of the spheres represented in the orrery is connected together and is part of a larger celestial or "analytical engine." Computers within the same solar system can be likened to individual planets or spheres. Compatible and connected with each other, they can communicate with each other—of course bound by the limits of time and space—through the use of modems or other data transfer systems (a disk, for example). Incompatible computer systems with unrelated operating systems represent solar systems whose elements are unconnected.

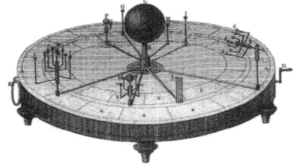

Illustration of an orrery from the *Iconographic Encyclopedia of Science, Literature, and Art, Systematically Arranged by J. G. Heck,* **translated from the German with additions and edited by Spenser F. Baird (New York: Rudolph Garrigue, 1851).**

In a non-linear system, whether the imaginative universe of science fiction or the reality of a hypertext system, the assumptions of a strictly linear universe no longer apply. Just as time and distance are redefined in our imagined science fiction universe, so to is the relationship between data and its meaning redefined in the hypertext and hypermedia universe.

The Tyranny of the Text

Historically, illustrations and pictorial material have been subsidiary to text. In a hypermedia environment, print no longer needs to dominate. The creation of extensive visual archive systems can transform the use of pictorial material. Visual explanation can supersede textual explanation when appropriate. In a hypertext environment where it becomes possible to easily present an illustrated film clip of a biological phenomenon, it becomes unnecessary to describe that phenomenon through text alone. Suppose, for example, that a naturalist decides that she wants to describe the motion of a running horse. A digitized film clip, inserted into a textual discussion, could be a preferable choice over a lengthy technical description. Slow motion pictures, diagrams and accompanying descriptions make the meaning of what it means for a horse to move suddenly much clearer than simply a text description.

It is interesting to note that with the Gutenberg revolution, the technology of the book made it possible to create and disseminate new ideas. Architecture was transformed, for example, by the creation of pattern books that could be cheaply reproduced and widely circulated. Symbolic representations, while certainly not new in their association with written language, were redefined and transformed. In 1668, for example, the Englishman John Wilkins wrote *An Essay towards a Real Character and a Philosophical Language* in which he presented series of calligraphic symbols to represent basic ideas.[10]

In fact, changes in typography and the symbolic function and presentation of text date back to the very earliest years of printing. Italic printing, for example, has its origins during this period. According to legend, the great Venetian Humanist and printer Aldus Mantius had developed italic type in order to be able to compress more text onto a single page. The design for italic was based on models of cursive handwriting then in use in the papal chancery.[11]

Italic typefaces are significant because they provide a standard typeface with a second dimension. Thus italic type accompanying a more linear roman face has imbedded in it a secondary message. In the title for this book, *Computing, Knowledge and Literacy: The Analytical Engine*, it may imply a specific meaning— i.e., a "book" or "a written or printed literary composition, esp. on consecutive sheets of paper bound together in a volume." Italics could be used to refer to an historical figure such as Cardinal Richelieu (1585–1642) by his nickname, *the gray eminence*. Italics can be used to *emphasize* a particular point, and so on.

The introduction and use of Italics may seem a trivial issue. In fact, it represents

an important example of how the new technology of print transformed the process of writing. Technically, italic handwriting was possible before the invention of print, but it was not widely used. When italic is written by calligraphers today, it simply represents a particular style of writing. *It is not typically used to offset or emphasize a specific point or concept in a text as is the case in this sentence.*

The introduction of new graphic means of presentation made possible by the print and typographic revolution of the fifteenth and sixteenth centuries reflected a radical reconceptualization of the meaning of text. The implication of these changes was profound. In her essay "Print Culture and Enlightenment Thought," Eizabeth Eisenstein asks us to consider what happened when reference books such as maps, gazetteers, atlases and lexicons underwent the shift from script culture to the print culture of the Reformation. Although such works are largely ignored by historianss, Eisenstein argues that "the activities of lexicographers, map publishers and globe makers during the first centuries after printing reverberated throughout the learned world."[12] The creation of Abraham Ortelius's multivolume atlas entitled the *Theatrum* in the sixteenth century and the seventeenth century *Grand Atlas* of Joan Blaeu represented the creation of a new type of work based on the collaborative collection of data. Knowledge was perceived and interpreted in new ways. In art and architecture new works were created such as Jan Vrederman de Vries's *Perspective*, Andrea Palladio's *I Quattro Libri dell'Architectura* and Sebastiano Serilo's *Tutte l'opere d'architectura et prospettiiva.*[13] Like the atlases, these literally provided a new way of looking at the world.

> In early Tudor England, Thomas Elyot expressed a preference for "figures and charts" over "hearing the rules of a science," which seems worth further thought. Although images were indispensable for prodding memory, a heavy reliance on verbal instruction had also been characteristic of communicating in the age of scribes. . . . After the advent of printing, visual aids multiplied, signs and symbols were codified; different kinds of iconographic and non-phonetic communication rapidly developed. The fact that printed picture books were newly designed by educational reformers for the purpose of instructing children and that drawing was considered an increasingly useful accomplishment by pedagogues also points to the need to think beyond the simple formula "image to word."[14]

New types of learning materials were introduced that were made possible by the introduction of text and visual material that worked in new and radical ways.

In works such as Johannn Amos Comenius's *Orbis Sensualium Pictus*, first

VIAGGI FATTI DA
VINETIA, ALLA TANA, IN PER=
SIA, IN INDIA, ET IN COSTANTI
NOPOLI: con la descrittione particolare di Città,
Luoghi, Siti, Costumi, et della PORTA del
gran TVRCO: & di tutte le intra=
te, spese, & modo di gouerno
suo, & della ultima im=
presa contra Por=
toghesi.

AL   DVS

IN VINEGIA   M.   D.   XLIII.

An example of **Aldine Italic** from a 1503 Aldine Press publication.

The outward and inward Senfes.

Senfus externi & interni.

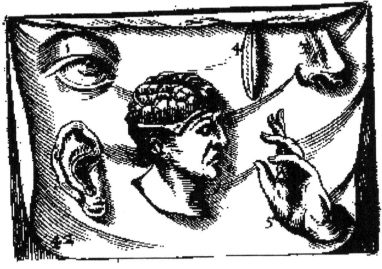

There are five outward Senfes;
The Eye 1.
feeth colours,
what is white or black,
green or blew,
red or yellow.
The Ear 2.
heareth Sounds,
both natural,
Voices and Words;
and artificial,
mufical Tunes.

Senfus externi funt quinque;
Oculus 1.
videt colores,
quid album vel atrum,
viride vel cœruleum,
rubrum aut luteum, &c.
Auris 2.
audit Sonos,
tum naturales,
Voces & Verba;
tum artificiales,
Tonos Muficos.

Sample page from Charles Hoole's 1672 English translation of Jan Amos Comenius's *Orbis Sensuliam Pictus.*

A page from Jan Vredeman de Vries's 1604 work *Perspective*.

published in 1658, detailed illustrations are integrated with virtually every major concept—thus providing a pictorial subtext for each concept included in the work. As a result, a literally new means of seeing and knowing was introduced. According to Eisenstein: "Within the Commonwealth of Learning it became increasingly fashionable to adopt the ancient Chinese maxim that a single picture was more valuable than many words."[15]

Seeing with a "third eye"—an "oculus Imaginationis"—became an important characteristic of seventeenth-century inquiry and thought.[16] Pictorial and symbolic forms organized and presented in the context of the new typographic culture created new ways of knowing and learning. Detailed visualization in the form of maps, architectural drawings and scientific illustrations increasingly became the norm. Fields such as medicine were tranformed with the first detailed and reproducible antatomical drawings.

A similar phenomenon is underway through the application and use of hypertext. In his 1963 essay "A Conceptual Framework for the Augmentation of Man's Intellect," the computer theorist Douglas C. Englebart proposed a device for "automated external symbol manipulation."[17] Using this device, the concepts an individual was manipulating could:

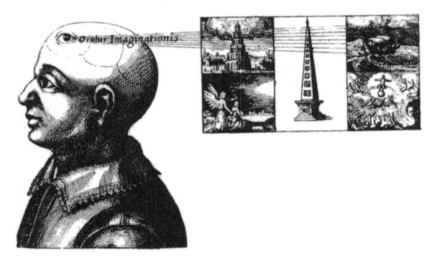

An illustration of the "third eye" or the "Oculus Imaginationis" from Robert Fludd's *Utriusque cosmi majoris ...* (Oppenheim: Johan-Theodor de Bry, 1621).

be arranged before his eyes, moved, stored, recalled, operated upon according to extremely complex rules—all in very rapid response to a minimum amount of information supplied by the human, by means of special cooperative technological devices. In the limit of what we might now imagine, this could be a computer, with which individuals could communicate rapidly and easily, coupled to a three-dimensional color display within which *extremely sophisticated images* could be constructed, the computer being able to execute a wide variety of processes on parts or all of these images in automatic response to human direction. The displays and processes could provide helpful services and could involve concepts not hitherto imagined.[18]

With a "mouse," this type of symbolic manipulation is precisely what occurs when one uses the icon system for a computer such as the Apple Macintosh or for a Windows environment on a computer. Symbols, such as the "trash can" on the Macintosh, for example, are manipulated, which represent much larger constructs and operations than their symbolic representations. Essentially, a "program" or function is contained within a symbol.

Symbolic representation of the type described above is by no means new—either to our own era or to the typographic culture that emerged in Europe during the fifteenth and sixteenth centuries. The use of iconic forms was widespread during the Middle Ages, whether as part of a manuscript, an altarpiece, or a stained glass window. During the Renaissance, various types of iconic forms were integrated with text—sometimes merging text with symbolic and stylized forms. A simple, but revolutionary example of this is the stylized logo/initials that the German artist Albrecht Dürer included on many of his etchings. Dürer's signature initials represent what must be one of the earliest uses of a "signature" on a work of art—perhaps a necessity resulting from the widespread circulation of his woodcuts and etchings and the need to have their origin identified. His stylized initials are in fact an icon, as well as a typographic form.

Examples of new iconic forms that are emerging as part of contemporary computer culture are as diverse as the Space Invader Warriors from the arcade game, Mario from the Nintendo game system, and the various icons and symbols included as part of the Macintosh system. Like Englebart, I believe that displays and processes will come into being through the use of hypertext and hypermedia involving "concepts not hitherto imagined."

An extremely simple example demonstrating this point would be the creation of electronic rebuses. A rebus is a representation of a word or phrase by pictures and/or symbols. The popular television game from the late 1950s *Concentration* used rebuses as the basis for its puzzles. Rebuses were widely used in children's games and activity books during the nineteenth century. Hypertext has the potential to reinvent the rebus as an animated form. Imagine a word processor that creates a rebus every time you write something. It might have a screen with a small narrow window at the base showing the word or sentence being written and its symbolic representation immediately above it. Animation and color could be added. Using a hypertext-based rebus writer one could write, "I saw the brown dog jump, and then jump even higher." The symbolic representation of the construction could include words, rebus constructions or symbols, and animations. Imagine such a system given to a grade-school child as a classroom word processor. It might also include a system for putting anything that is written on the computer into a synthesized speech package that could be played back, or, as yet another window, present whatever is written in a phonetic form such as the Initial Teaching Alphabet. Using hypertext techniques, this is not only feasible to propose, but relatively easy to execute.

Rebus from *Mother Goose Hieroglyphicks* (**Boston: Brown and Taggard, c. 1860**).

A computerized rebus writer is relatively primitive compared to what will probably emerge as part of hypertext systems during the next ten to fifteen years. It is perfectly plausible to imagine symbolic/iconic writing systems being developed for the composition of poetry. The sort of elaborate word and special textual presentations that are found in the work of poets such as E. E. Cummings will probably go through a further process of evolution. Verbs will literally become active—when appropriate—migrating across the computer screen. Exclamation points will explode as they emphasize their point. A word like *unfold* may literally do what its says. Or *disappear*, may literally disappear. *Concave* may literally be concave. Sound will be incorporated into textual and visual materials. Thus, the reader will not only see the "brown dog" jump higher and higher, but he or she will literally be able to hear him bark at the moon as well. Text, visual representations and sound will combine together to give new meaning to what it is to be literate.

CONCAVE

Are prognostications such as these simply futuristic rhetoric? In fact, they are clearly possible even today with the technology currently available on a sophisticated desktop computer system. How quickly such hypertext systems come into use, however, will depend upon issues related to cultural lag and generational resistance to new technological forms. In this context, the educational philosopher Robert McClintock has pointed out that technical systems have remarkably long periods of development. The Eiffel Tower, which represented a new architectural technology of steel and iron structures, is over one hundred years old, yet the architectural systems it fathered (skyscrapers, elevators, etc.) are still in the process of evolution. Similarly, automobile and air transportation, radio and television are still developing to new levels of sophistication.[19] According to McClintock, common but complex technologies such as these typically "require one to two hundred years for the development of their full potentialities, perhaps even longer."[20] In this context, the computer and more specifically, microcomputers and hypertext, are very new technologies.

Digital versus Analog Universes

Thomas Kuhn argues in *The Structure of Scientific Revolutions* that different scientific paradigms can coexist with each other. A paradigm that can be defined as a pattern, an example or a model represents a way of organizing and interpreting the world. Established paradigms carry a great deal of weight and are difficult to supersede with new paradigms. Custom, familiarity and cost are just a few of the factors that mitigate against the rapid adoption and assimilation of a new paradigm.[21]

Kuhn argues that scientists typically work with a dominant paradigm until enough anomalies or contradictions appear in a field that force them to consider a new model or perspective. An example would be Newtonian theories of motion and matter dominating the field of physics until the work of Einstein at the beginning of this century. Yet scientists, rather than immediately embracing Einstein's work, took more than a generation to fully integrate his theories into the scientific community.

This same phenomenon can be seen in the case of archiving text and photographic materials. Microfilm was invented by the Englishman John Benjamin Dancer in 1852. The first microfilm reader, the Fiskescope, was invented by the American Bradley A. Fiske in 1919. In 1939 Elgin G. Fassel, of Milwaukee, Wisconsin, introduced the first mass card filing system—essentially the modern microfiche. By the 1960s microfilm and microfiche had become the main archival storage technology used in the culture.

Microfilm and microfiche is a technology that is clearly obsolete. As a paradigm or a model it has been superseded by new models of digital storage. Hypertext and hypermedia are in fact the next logical stage of development for the organization and archiving of printed and pictorial information. Yet despite its practicality and its overwhelming superiority to microfilm and microfiche, its universal adoption and use of hypermedia by business, government and research institutions will take at least a half generation, if not a generation, to complete.

The reasons for this are explained by Kuhn. The investment in the old technology (i. e., microfilm readers, collections of film and fiche, etc.) is so great that it cannot be easily discarded. In addition, existing patterns of familiarity make it difficult for individuals to easily adopt the new technology. Essentially, the new system will not be adopted until it becomes so overwhelmingly disadvantageous to hold on to the old technology that change is finally undertaken.

Significantly, the transition between the use of microfilm and microfiche and hypertext systems is even more marked by the deep structures involved. Not only is there a fundamental difference between the two technologies, but also between the foundations upon which they organize and reproduce knowledge. Fiche and microfilm systems, like audio recordings and books, are analog systems. Computers, microcomputers, laser disk systems (compact audio and visual systems) are digital systems. The difference between the assumptions and technologies underlying each are profound. As Robert McClintock explains:

> Digital technologies do not transmit one thing that is analogous to another, the real matter in question. Rather, a digital technology transmits exact, or nearly exact, values, as precisely as these can be represented in binary code. . . . . The key to digital technology, compared with analog, is the digital lack of ambiguity: It deals with successive states, either-or conditions in which a circuit is either off or on. In contrast, the analog technology deals endlessly with the torturing indefinite in which each successive state differs from its predecessor by a nearly infinitesimal increment. The analog approximates one whole with another; the digital samples the whole and recreates it from that sampling.[22]

In this context, digital technology represents a paradigm shift. The storage, structure and logic of stored information have been profoundly altered. As Norbert Wiener observed in his work *The Human Use of Human Beings* in reference to the work of the American scientist Willard Gibbs, entropy, as demonstrated by the second law of thermodynamics, has a tendency to increase in our universe:

> As entropy increases, the universe, and all closed systems in the universe, tend naturally to deteriorate and lose their distinctiveness, to move from the least to the most probable state, from a state of organization and differentiation in which distinctions and forms exist, to a state of chaos and sameness.[23]

Analog systems have a much greater tendency towards entropy than digital systems. Digital systems "recreate" an object or thing from a binary code. As long as the binary code is preserved and not allowed to degenerate, an exact copy of the original phenomenon is reproduced. Thus with a laser audio disk there should be no difference between the master disk and the digital copy. A recording of Glenn Gould playing Bach's *Goldberg Variations* is virtually the same on the digital master and the compact laser audio disks that are produced from it. In marked contrast, an analog recording involves an analog master, which reproduces the sounds from the recording studio as a series of variations that are recorded on the surface of a medium such as plastic or vinyl. A rough analog model is created by the recording, which is then used to press copies. These analog messages are then translated through a stylus and amplified.

An analog system is subject to relatively rapid deterioration and entropy. An analog record played five thousand times, no matter what quality of equipment is being used, will almost certainly wear out. Distortion will be so profound that the original data of the recording will be totally lost. In contrast, the digital system should provide a sound with precisely the same quality as when it was first played.

Analog and digital represent systems subject to different physical laws. Entropy is not a significant issue in digital systems compared with analog systems. McClintock believes that the ramifications underlying analog versus digital systems are profound.

> For instance, copyright laws seem to break down in the digital environments because the familiar dynamics of reproduction do not seem to hold. Copies in the familiar analog realm, are costly to make and at best approximate, leaving clear traces of what is original and what is the copy. In the digital realm, copies are nearly costless, they are often indistinguishable from the original, assuming some real meaning to "original" can in fact be attached to something substantial.[24]

In addition, with digitalization "computer bits migrate merrily," escaping from their traditional analog means of transmission. A movie, phone call, audio recording or book become translatable into each other. Each may be sent by fiber optic, coaxial cable, microwave, satellite, tape or disk—just to name a few of the mediums available.[25]

In my earlier work, *Beyond the Gutenberg Galaxy: Microcomputers and the Emergence of Post-Typographic Culture*, I argued that as a result of the introduction of microcomputers we are seeing the emergence of a post-typographic culture.[26] Post-typographic culture is a digital culture. It brings with it, like all new technologies, the potential to create a new human environment. As Marshall McLuhan explained:

> Any technology tends to create a new human environment. Script and papyrus created the social environment we think of in connection with the empires of the ancient world. The stirrup and the wheel created unique environments of enormous scope. Technological environments are not merely passive containers of people but are active processes that reshape people and other technologies alike.[27]

The introduction of digital technology represents the crossing of a new frontier. We are entering a new phase of our cultural history. According to McClintock, in doing so "we have initiated an irreversible action in cultural history."[28] A frontier has been crossed that "is not simply technical, but deeply cultural."[29] Hypertext is the most profound manifestation of this new post-typographic or digital culture.

Culture can be defined as a "vast store of externalized memory."[30] It is memory put into things outside of the human brain, into books, architecture, paintings, photographs and paintings to name just a few examples. Up until now, the various means of coding information outside of the brain have functioned very differently. The codes of writing are different from those of pictorial representation, which in turn differ from those of sculpture, architecture, still photography or film.[31] As a result, the domains of culture have been divided into widely diverse systems of storage and retrieval, each with its own rules.

A hypertext system can "link" or unify different cultural codes through a common digital or binary structure. Through the use of various algorithms the expression of a formula can be transformed into a graph, a pictorial representation or a piece of music. Phenomena expressed through different codes are reunified in a single unitary digital logic. Hyperlinks are like the threads of a tapestry that connects its diverse sections. As a result:

> All culture can be coded so that it can be operated on with digital computers, and the operation of digital computers is such that it will not only allow for the storage and retrieval of information through objects external to our minds, but will also permit the intelligent processing of that information in those external objects.[32]

The fundamental rule of digital culture comes down to being that "insofar as we can express something in binary code, we can recreate it."[33] According to McClintock, the implications of this are that as we learn to specify things in binary or digital code "we can recreate in digital technology the forms of intelligence so specified."[34] In doing so we have initiated ourselves into a culture based upon intelligence rather than remembrance.[35]

Hypertext and hypermedia systems are part of this new or "post-typographic culture."[36] It is critical that as we move towards a more comprehensive use and expansion of hypertext and hypermedia systems, we understand their implications for control, education and freedom. Hypertext, as computers in general, represents a value-laden technology. As we adopt hypertext systems—a fact the author assumes is almost inevitable—we must recognize that they, like the computer, are not neutral.

I strongly agree with J. David Bolter, who has argued that just as it makes sense to examine Plato and pottery together in order to understand Greek culture, Descartes and the mechanical clock in order to understand Europe in the seventeenth and eighteenth centuries, so too does it make "sense to regard the computer as a technological paradigm for the science, the philosophy, even the art of the coming generation."[37]

The idea of mankind's uniqueness depending on his technological ability is by no means a new or original idea. Man as toolmaker—*homo faber*—is an essential character of his uniqueness in the animal kingdom. Technology is essentially the source of much of what makes us unique as human beings. It is also a source of many of our problems. While the basic character of human beings probably has not changed significantly from the ancient era to the present, technology has the capacity to amplify the characteristics of humanity to an unprecedented degree. It is not a question of whether or not we are more good or evil when compared to previous generations, but the degree to which we can exercise, as a result of access to specific technology, actions that are good or evil. In the following chapters I will explore in more detail the potential of the computer, and more specifically, the elements of the Analytical Engine to create good or evil, as well transform the meaning of literacy and education.

Notes

1. George P. Landow, "Hypertext in Literary Education, Criticism, and Scholarship," *Computers and the Humanities*, vol. 23 (1989), p. 173.

2. *Ibid.*, pp. 173–174.

3. *Ibid.*, p. 174.

4. In hypertext parlance this is referred to as activating a "hot spot" or "hot word."

5. *The Holy Bible: Containing the Old and New Testaments: Translated from the original Tongues Being the Version Set Forth A.D. 1611* (New York: Thomas Nelson & Sons, 1952), p. 1.

6. George P. Landow, "The Rhetoric of Hypermedia: Some Rules for Authors," *Journal of Computing in Higher Education*, Vol. 1 , No. 1 (Spring 1989), p. 39.

7. Edward Barrett, ed., *Text, ConText, and Hypertext: Writing with and for the Computer* (Cambridge: MIT Press, 1988), p. ix.

8. Edward Barrett, ed., *The Society of Text: Hypertext, Hypermedia, and the Social Construction of Information* (Cambridge, MA: MIT Press, 1989).

9. Ted Nelson describes several different types of hypertext. "Chunk style hypertext" involves the reader moving through one "chunk" and the selecting the next "chunk." "Compound text" or "windowing text" involves materials being viewed and combined with other materials. Nelson explains that a good way of visualizing a "compound text" "is a set of windows to original materials from the compound text themselves." Extending this notion, Nelson develops the idea of *"windowing hypertext"* in which "nonsequential writings—hypertexts—window to other stored materials."

    Nelson argues convincingly that hypertext much more closely imitates how ideas are actually structured in the human mind than sequential forms of language and text:

    > *The structure of ideas* is never sequential; and indeed, our thought processes are not very sequential either. True, only a few thoughts at a time pass across the central screen of the mind; but you consider a thing, your thoughts crisscross it constantly, reviewing first one connection, then another. Each new idea is compared with many parts of the whole picture, or with some mental visualization of the whole picture itself.

    See: Nelson, *Literary Machines*, pp. 1/15–1/16.

10. John Wilkins, *An Essay Towards a Real Character and a Philosophical Language* (London, 1868). Reprinted, edited by R. C. Alston, English Linguistics 1500–1800, no. 119. (Menston, England: Scolar Press, 1968). John Wilkins and his ideas are explored in the Neal Stephenson's novels *Cryptonomicon* (New York: Avon Press, 1999) and *Quicksilver* (The Baroque Cycle, Vol. 1) (New York: Harper Collins, 2003).

11. Jan Van White, *Graphic Design for the Electronic Age: The Manual for Traditional and Desktop Publishing* (New York: Waton-Guptill Publications, 1988), p. 37.

12. Elizabeth Eisenstein, *Print Culture and Enlightenment Thought* (Chapel Hill, NC: Hanes Foundation, 1986), p. 4.

13. See: Jan Vredeman de Vries, *Perspective*, with a new introduction by Adolf K. Placzek (New York: Dover Publications, 1968), reprint of the 1604 work published by

Henricus Hondius in Leiden; Andrea Palladio, *The Four Books of Architecture*, with a new introduction by Adolf K. Placzek (New York: Dover Publications, 1965), reprint of the 1738 English edition of Palladio's work first published in Venice in 1570; and Sebastiano Serlio, *The Five Books of Architecture* (New York: Dover Publications, 1982), reprint of the 1611 English edition of the work first published in Venice in 1537.

14. Elizabeth Eisenstein, *The Printing Revolution in Early Modern Europe* (New York: Cambridge University Press, 1983), p. 37.

15. *Ibid.*

16. *Ibid.*, p. 36.

17. Englebart, Douglas, "A Conceptual Framework for the Augmentation of Man's Intellect." In P. W. Howerton and D. C. Weeks, *Vistas in Information Handling: Vol. 1. The Augmentation of Man's Intellect by Machine* (Washington, DC: Spartan Books, 1963), p. 14.

18. *Ibid.*

19. Robert O. McClintock, "Marking the Second Frontier," *Teachers College Record*, Vol. 89, No. 3 (Spring 1988), pp. 346–347.

20. *Ibid.*, p. 347. A similar argument is made by Tom Forester that:

> human and social factors have consistently delayed major technological and communication "revolutions." It has taken much longer than popularly imagined, he says, for society to assimilate innovations such as TV and the telephone. As with the computer, TVS and telephones were initially acclaimed as remarkable, "revolutionary technologies, but their penetration rate was surprisingly slow and their dissemination to the masses was delayed, chiefly by the Establishment who feared their potential for the radical disruption of the existing social structure: "the history of the technologies of information reveals a gradual, uncataclysmic progress. No telecommunication technology of itself or in aggregate suggests revolutionary development. On the contrary, each of them can be seen as a technological response to certain social relations which, at least in the West, have remained basically unchanged during the entire industrial period."

See the editor's introduction to Forester, Tom (ed.), *Computers in the Human Context*, (Massachusetts: MIT Press, 1989), p. 8.

21. Thomas Kuhn, *The Structure of Scientific Revolutions* (Chicago: University of Chicago Press, 1962).

22. McClintock, p. 346.

23. Norbert Wiener, *The Human Use of Human Beings: Cybernetics and Society* (New York: Avon Books, 1967), p. 20.

24. McClintock, p. 348.

25. Stewart Brand, *The Media Lab: Inventing the Future at M.I.T.* (New York: Penguin Books, 1988), p. 18.

26. Eugene F. Provenzo Jr., *Beyond the Gutenberg Galaxy: Microcomputers and the Emergence of Post-Typographic Culture* (New York: Teachers College Press, 1986).

27. Marshall McLuhan, *Understanding Media: The Extensions of Man* (New York: Mentor Books, 1964), p. 1v.

28. McClintock, p. 249.

29. *Ibid.*

30. *Ibid.*, p. 350.

31. *Ibid.*, p. 350.

32. McClintock, p. 350.

33. *Ibid.*

34. *Ibid.*, p. 351.

35. *Ibid.*

36. See: *Provenzo*, op. cit.

37. J. David Bolter, *Turning's Man: Western Culture in the Computer Age* (Chapel Hill: USniversity of North Carolina Press, 1984), p. xii.

Chapter 3

The Dream of Encyclopedic Knowledge

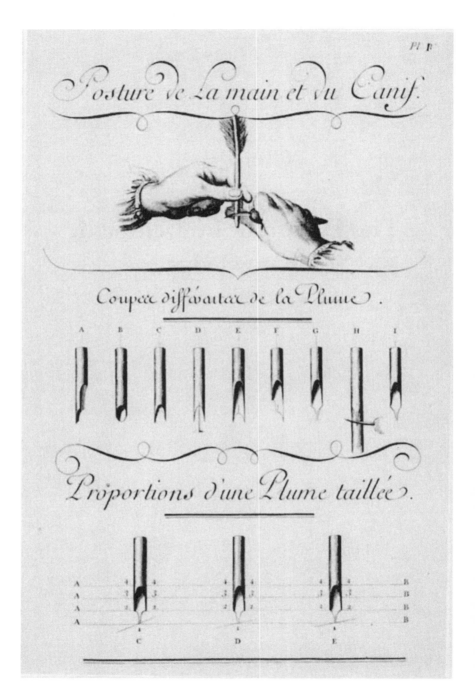

Plate titled "L'art d'écrire" in *Encyclopédie, ou Dictionnaire des sciences, des arts et des méiers* (ca. 1762-77).

In his 1945 essay "As We May Think" Vannevar Bush argued that in the not too distant future new types of encyclopedias would be created that would have a:

> mesh of associative trails running through them, ready to be dropped into the Memex and there amplified. The lawyer has at his fingertips the associated opinions and decisions of his whole experience and of the experience of friends and authorities. The patent attorney has on call the millions of issued patents, with familiar trails to every point of his client's interest. The physician puzzled by a patient's reaction strikes the trail established in studying an earlier similar case, and runs rapidly through analogous case histories, with side references to the classics for the pertinent anatomy and histology. . . . The historian, with a vast chronological account of a people parallels it with a skip trail which stops only on the salient items, and can follow at any time contemporary trails which lead him all over civilization at a particular epoch.[1]

Bush's description of new forms of encyclopedias is now a reality. Patent records are now available online that include hypertext and hypermedia functions. Medical students dissect cadavers with the assistance of hypermedia reference systems. Historians working at the Library of Congress review vast photographic and text records dealing with American culture and society using hypertext and hypermedia systems.

With the emergence of the Internet and the World Wide Web, these sources are available not only in libraries and research centers but anywhere that has a computer with access to the Internet. We have realized Bush's dream of creating vast associative trails and indexes.

A demonstration of this is the fact that while I am writing this text, I am also connected through my computer to the Internet and the World Wide Web. Using the search engine Google I have searched for Web sites that are related to the work of the poet and illustrator William Blake (1757–1827). Blake is of interest to me because of his remarkable artistry and his experimentation with the use of text forms in poetry. Literally dozens of sites are available to me, including *The William Blake Archive*, a collaborative project of the Library of Congress, the National Endowment of the Humanities, the University of Virginia and the University of North Carolina (www.blakearchive.org). Under the direction of Morris Eaves at the University of Rochester, Robert Essick at the University of California, Riverside, and Joseph Viscomi at the University of North Carolina, Chapel Hill, the project involves the creation of an electronic archive that includes fifty-five key copies of Blake's nineteen illuminated books. Begin in 1996, it continues to be added to on a regular basis—growing and evolving as does the field of Blake studies. Over three thousand images are included in the archive, two thirds from Blake's illuminated manuscripts and the remaining third from Blake's paintings, drawings and engravings.

Included as part of the archive are extensive links to the works of other Blake scholars, as well as links, or associative trails, to related sites on the World Wide Web. Using the conference system *Blake Online*, I can leave messages or inquiries for Blake scholars. Key primary documents, as well as bibliographical sources, can be accessed, printed and even electronically downloaded to my computer.[2]

The "Ancient of Days" by William Blake.

A new type of digital archive has been created—one that is remarkably dynamic and relatively easy to revise. It is creating an invisible network or a universe of scholars, connected together on a worldwide basis through the Internet. It is Bush's dream of associative trails and indexing come true. In this context (as I will argue in the following chapter), I believe that the Internet and the World Wide Web simply represent another permutation of hypertext and hypermedia, which when combined together are part of that larger phenomenon of what I term the "Difference Engine."

The Dream of Encyclopedic Knowledge

The desire to create and use vast encyclopedias of knowledge is by no means a new phenomenon. The ancient library founded in Alexandria during the reign of the Greek Emperor Ptolemy was perhaps the earliest attempt in Western society to develop encyclopedic systems of information. Each time a merchant ship arrived in the port, inquiries were made as to whether there were books on board. Whenever this was the case, the original was taken to the library and copied, a "fair copy" being returned to the owner.[3] Encyclopedic collections can be found in the Middle Ages with the work of individuals such as Isadore of Seville, and in the Renaissance with the work of figures such as Francis Bacon.

The modern encyclopedia movement dates largely from eighteenth-century France and the work of the Encyclopedists. Begun in 1746 by a group of French publishers as a translation of the English *Cyclopedia* by Ephraim Chambers, the work was soon expanded far beyond its original purpose. As conceived by its editor Denis Diderot, the *Encyclopedie* became an extraordinary attempt to record all of the knowledge of science and industry.[4] The final volumes which appeared in 1765, together with their illustrative plates which were completed two years later, were intended to be a "sanctuary where the knowledge of man is protected from time and revolutions."[5]

At the very center of the *Encyclopedie* was the rationalist assumption that it was possible to conceive of a reasoned and connected system of knowledge. As D'Alembert explained in *The Preliminary Discourse*, which outlined in detail the scope and purpose of the project:

> . . . it is readily apparent that the sciences and the arts are mutually supporting, and that consequently there is a chain that binds them together. But, if it is often difficult to reduce each particular science or art to a small number of rules or general notions, it is no less difficult to encompass the infinitely varied branches of human knowledge in a truly unified system.[6]

Much like the deconstructionist movement in literature, the French encyclopedists argued that implicit in the encyclopedia project was:

> the genealogy and the filtration of the parts of our knowledge, the causes that brought the various parts of our knowledge into being, and the characteristics that distinguish them. In short we must go back to the origin and generation of our ideas.[7]

Reading D'Alembert, one can see a rationale at work similar to that underlying many of the current assumptions about hypertext and hypermedia systems. Information and the knowledge that results from it can be arranged in a natural order and communicated through the process of Logic, which:

. . . teaches how to arrange ideas in the most natural order, how to link them together in the most direct sequence, how to break up those which include too large a number of simple ideas, how to view ideas in all their facets, and finally how to present them to others in a form that makes them easy to grasp.[8]

The desire manifested by the encyclopedists to organize knowledge in its "most natural order" and "to link them together in the most direct sequence" was not an isolated phenomenon of the eighteenth century. In the American colonies it can clearly be seen at work in the thinking of Thomas Jefferson, whose organization for his personal library suggests many of the major characteristics associated with hypertext and hypermedia systems.

Hypertext Principles and Thomas Jefferson's Library

Throughout his life, among the major interests of Thomas Jefferson was the development of his library. Jefferson began collecting books as a young man. His first library was destroyed by fire in 1770. Despite this loss, by 1783 Jefferson noted that he owned a total of 2,640 volumes. Adding to his collection throughout the rest of his life, Jefferson's library numbered 6,700 volumes by 1815.[9]

Jefferson's collection of books was encyclopedic in nature. His intention was to pull together, into a single collection, the whole of recorded knowledge. His library was sold in its entirety to Congress in 1815 to replace the books that had been burned by the British in 1814. It became the core collection for the modern Library of Congress.[10]

Jefferson's library was carefully arranged by him into the categories of Memory, Reason and Imagination based upon Francis Bacon's work *The Advancement of Learning*. Memory was further divided into four parts: natural (including information about technology and information based on inanimate and animate things), civil, ecclesiastical and literary. Reason was divided into divine, natural and civil, and Imagination into narrative, representative (drama) and parabolical (allegory).[11] Jefferson made various modifications and additions to Bacon's system. Most significant was the addition of forty-four chapters, which included new categories that were not known in Bacon's time, such as chemistry. Jefferson's system of classification was deliberately flexible in order to take into account new areas of knowledge and discovery.[12]

When Jefferson offered his library for sale to the Congress in 1814, he included with it his catalogue and classification system. Unfortunately his collection was not maintained in its original order after the library purchased the collection. As he explained in a letter to Joseph Cabell:

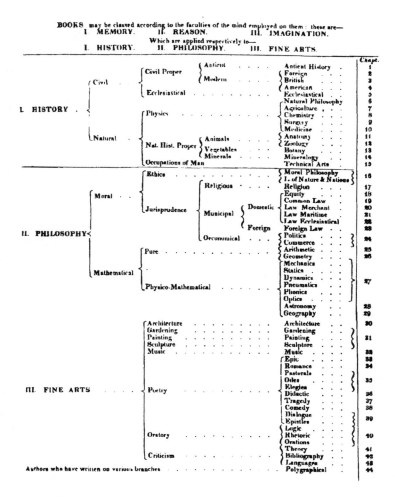

Jefferson's classification system for his library as it appears in the Catalogue of the Library of the United States (Washington, D.C.: Printed by Jonathan Elliot, 1815).

The form of the catalogue has been much injured in the publication; for although they have preserved my division into chapters, they have reduced the books in each chapter to alphabetical order, instead of the chronological or analytical arrangements I had given them.[13]

In fact, Jefferson's organization of his library represented a primitive hypertext system. In order to understand this system, one must understand how he organized and shelved his collection at Monticello and at his second home, Poplar Forest. According to Gary Wills:

For maximum economy of space, Jefferson fitted his walls with boxes that formed shelves, putting books of the same size on the same shelf, so that no space was wasted between the tops of the books and the tops of the boxes. But he kept a master list that showed the order of the book regardless of the size, and he could move his eye up and down the shelves stacked above each other, to trace the hierarchy of books on any subject. When his boxes were shipped off to Congress, he sent the master list, but the librarian did not grasp its importance for Jefferson. The variations in the size of the books when they were taken from the boxes and put directly on shelves made it look like things were random within the large categories, so at the Library of Congress, they were entered alphabetically by authors within the subject groupings.[14]

Jefferson's catalogue and shelf order for his library was based on the interconnectedness and relatedness of their subjects. Authors such as Alfred Bestor have argued that in this sense, Jefferson's catalogue provided a "blueprint" for his mind.[15] In the development of his library classification system he implicitly understood the point made by Vannevar Bush over 150 years later in 1945 when he argued that:

Our ineptitude in getting at the record is largely caused by the artificiality of systems of indexing. When data of any sort are placed in storage, they are filed alphabetically or numerically, and information is found (when it is) by tracing it down from subclass to subclass. It can be in only one place, unless duplicates are used; one has to have rules as to which path will locate it, and the rules are cumbersome. Having found one item, moreover, one has to emerge from the system and re-enter on a new path.[16]

Bush, like Jefferson, recognized that the human mind does not work according to alphabetical or numerical lists, but instead by means of association:

With one item in its grasp, it snaps instantly to the next that is suggested by the association of thoughts, in accordance with some intricate web of trails carried by the cells of the brain.[17]

This idea of associative indexing represents the fundamental idea underlying hypertext and hypermedia—and also represents the type of thinking that went into Jefferson's personal organization of knowledge.

The Great Books of the Western World as a Hypertext System

Attempts to make available associated types of knowledge represent a fundamental aspect of encyclopedic thought. In the twentieth century, for example, the *Great Books of the Western World* under the editorship of Robert M. Hutchins attempted to draw together the complete and unexpurgated works of the most influential thinkers included in Western thought. The set, including 443 works by 74 authors, was seen by Hutchins "as a great conversation. . . . a conversation that has gone on for twenty-five centuries."[18]

Among the most interesting aspects of the development of the Great Books series was the development of the *Synopticon*. The *Synopticon*, according to Hutchins, was:

begin as an index and then turned into a means of helping the reader find paths through the books, has ended, in addition to making these contributions as a tool for reference, research, and study, as a preliminary summation of the issues around which the Great Conversation has revolved, together with indications of the course of the debate at this moment. Once again, the *Synopticon* argues no case and presents no point of view. It will not interpret any book to the reader; it will not tell him which author is right and which wrong on any question. It simply supplies him with suggestions as to how he may conveniently peruse the study of any important topic through the range of Western intellectual history.[19]

The philosopher Mortimer Adler was primarily responsible for the development of the *Synopticon*. Including 102 categories or "chapters," topics dealt with in the Index were as diverse as "Temperance," "Sign and Symbol," and "Slavery." Under the category of "Poetry," for example, there are nine major topics, including: "The nature of poetry: its distinction from other arts," "The origin and development of poetry: the materials of myth and legend," etc.[20] Under the category of "The nature of poetry: its distinction from other arts," are references to authors such as Plato, Aristotle, Lucretius, Epictetus, Augustine, Aquinas, Dante, Hobbes, Montaigne, Shakespeare, Cervantes, Bacon, Descartes, Milton, Pascal, Swift, Fielding, Kant, Hegel, Goethe, Darwin, Dostoevsky and Freud.[21]

Implicit in Adler's *Synopticon* is a desire to create links between different authors writing on the same or related topics. In this sense, as the work's editor Adler assumes the role of trailblazer. In Bush's Memex system, such individuals played a crucial role:

There is a new profession of trail blazers, those who find delight in the task of establishing useful trails through the enormous mass of the common record. The inheritance from the master becomes not only his additions to the world's record, but for his disciples the entire scaffolding by which they were erected.[22]

Significantly, while an editor or "trailblazer" such as Adler may demonstrate objectivity in his work, the selection of materials—despite Hutchins's arguments—represents a point of view or specific perspective.

The *Synopticon* is an encyclopedic document that has enormous potential, but is physically cumbersome and difficult to use. To use it effectively, you need to be able to quickly compare different passages, to line them up next to each other, and to be able to record and store them. The print/text format for such a document is highly limiting. Its true potential is realized in a hypertext format. It can be argued that the *Synopticon* is in fact a hypertext system without a computer or engine to drive it.

Hypertext and Hypermedia as Encyclopedic Systems

Hypertext and hypermedia are by definition encyclopedic systems. As such, they make possible the presentation of data in new ways in terms of text, visual and auditory sources. Hypertext and hypermedia systems when delivered through the Internet and the World Wide Web—have the potential to function as equalizers in our society by making available on a wide-spread basis massive visual and text data bases, whose sources could only be laboriously tracked down in our great libraries and research centers. Suddenly, vast encyclopedic sources are available with accompanying tools that allow their manipulation and use. For over thirty years as a researcher and scholar I have been visiting the Library of Congress's Prints and Photographic Division, as well as its Rare Book Collection. Now, through the library's *American Memory Collection* (http://lcweb.loc.gov/amhome.html) I have direct access to many of the collections that in the past I could only look at by actually visiting Washington, D.C. Manuscripts from the Folklore Division of the WPA Federal Writer's Project, photographs of the Civil War by Mathew Brady, as well as pamphlets and photographs on the history of African-American culture from Daniel A. P Murray Collection are now easily available to me.

Many of these documents are linked to other sources and archives. While this is particularly helpful for an experienced scholar and researcher like myself, its even more important that these materials are now available not just to researchers, but to the general public as well. One would hope that access to sources such as these would lead to a renaissance of interest on the part of school children and adults in hyperlinked sources of information.

The growth of the Internet and the World Wide Web is part of a larger expansion of knowledge and information access that has been going on since at least the Second World War. In "How We May Think," Vannevar Bush, for example, argued that even in 1945, publication had:

> been extended far beyond our present ability to make real use of the record. The summation of human experience is being expanded at a prodigious rate and the means we use for threading through the consequent maze to the momentarily important item is the same as was used in the days of square-rigged ships.[23]

Using primitive microfilm systems, Bush unrealistically proposed the compression of a library of a million volumes into one end of a desk—all of the books and print materials ever produced into a space small enough so that it "could be lugged off in a moving van."[24] In fact, digital technology and more specifically the Internet—rather than microfilm technology—makes such a proposition clearly feasible, on an even larger scale than that proposed by Bush.

* * *

Where do we stand with all of this? Marshall McLuhan wrote over a quarter of a century ago that:

> We are today as far into the electric age as the Elizabethans had advanced into the typographical and mechanical age. And we are experiencing the same confusions and indecisions which they had felt when living simultaneously in two contrasted forms of society and experience.[25]

Recent developments such as Google's *Google Books Library Project* (http://books.google.com/googlebooks/library.html) represents an attempt to develop a world-wide library, one which will eventually make virtually all copyright free books available online, as well millions of other works whose use has been obtained from publishers and authors. As they explain at their website for the project:

> The Library Project's aim is simple: make it easier for people to find relevant books—specifically, books they wouldn't find any other way such as those that are out of print—while carefully respecting authors' and publishers' copyrights. Our ultimate goal is to work with publishers and libraries to create a comprehensive, searchable, virtual card catalog of all books in all languages that helps users discover new books and publishers discover new readers.[26]

This is the realization of the Great Library at Alexandria, H. G. Well's World Library and Vannevar Bush's Memex. The dream of encyclopedic knowledge on a worldwide basis has, at last, been realized. The related implications are profound. Vast encyclopedic systems based on hypertext and hypermedia principles have the potential to redefine how we organize and control information. We are already at a point where traditional knowledge and information systems are in the process of being redefined, while we are still establishing the ground rules for a post-typographic culture.

Notes

1. Vannevar Bush, "As We May Think," in *Computer-Supported Cooperative Work: A Book of Readings*, ed. Irene Greif (San Mateo, CA: Morgan Kaufmann Publishers, Inc., 1988), p. 32.

2. *The Institute for Advanced Technologies in the Humanities* at the University of Virginia (http://jefferson.village.virginia.edu/), one of the sponors of *The William Blake Archive*, has dozens of scholarly hypermedia projects of the type being discussed. *The Complete Writings and Pictures of Dante Gabriel Rossetti* (www.rossettiarchive.org/), for example, is "a hypertextual instrument designed to facilitate the scholarly study of Dante Gabriel Rossetti, the painter, designer, writer, and translator who was, according to both John Ruskin and Walter Pater, the most important and original artistic force in the second half of the nineteenth century in Great Britain." *The Valley of the Shadow* project (http://valley.vcdh.virginia.edu/) provides a highly detailed historical archive on a Northern (Franklin County Pennsylvania) and Southern community (Augusta County, Virginia) during the Civil War. It includes "thousands of original letters and diaries, newspapers and speeches, census and church records. *The Sixties Project* (www3.iath.virginia.edu/sixties/) provides a means of networking scholars for the purposes of doing collaborative research, as well as primary and secondary sources for research on the social, cultural and political movements of the 1960s. At a site like *The Dickinson Archive* (www.emilydickinson.org/) visitors are given access to a massive electronic archive of original writings and resources about the American poetess Emily Dickinson. In the case of the *The Samantabhadra Collection* (www.thdl.org/collections/literature/nyingma.html) visitors to the sites are provided access to an electronic archive focused on the analysis, interpretation, and translation of Tibetan literature in the Nyingma tradition.

3. James Westfall Thompson, *Ancient Libraries* (Berkeley, CA: University of California Press, 1940), p. 23.

4. *Encyclopedia Selections*, trans. Nelly Hoyt and Thomas Cassirer Schwab, "The Library of Liberal Arts," no. 223 (Indianapolis: Bobbs-Merrill Company, Inc., 1965) pp. vii–ix.

5. Jean le Rond d'Alembert, *Preliminary Discourse to the Encyclopedia of Diderot*, trans. R. Schwab, "The Library of Liberal Arts," no. 89 (Indianapolis: Bobbs-Merrill Company, Inc., 1963), p. 121.

6. *Ibid.*, p. 5.

7. *Ibid.*

8. *Ibid.*, p. 30.

9. *Thomas Jefferson's Library: A Catalog with the Entries in His Own Order*, ed. James Gilreath and Douglas L. Wilson (Washington, DC: Library of Congress, 1989), p. 1.

10. *Ibid.*, pp. 1–2.

11. *Ibid.*, p. 2.

12. *Ibid.*

13. Quoted by Gilreath and Wilson, *Ibid.*

14. Gary Wills, Review of *Jefferson's Literary Commonplace Book* (ed. Douglas L.

Wilson), *The New Republic*, January 22, 1990, p. 42.

15. Gilreath and Wilson, *Thomas Jefferson's Library*, p. 8.

16. Bush, "How We May Think," p. 29.

17. *Ibid.*

18. Robert M. Hutchins, *The Great Conversation: The Substance of a Liberal Education* (Chicago: Encyclopedia Britannica, Inc., 1952), p. xx.

19. *Ibid.*, p. xxv.

20. Mortimer J. Adler, *The Great Ideas: A Synopticon of Great Books of the Western World*, Vol. 2 (Chicago: Encyclopedia Britannica, Inc., 1952), p. 409.

21. *Ibid.*, p. 410.

22. Bush, "How We May Think," p. 32.

23. Bush, "How We May Think," p. 19.

24. *Ibid.*, p. 22.

25. Marshall McLuhan, *Understanding Media: The Extensions of Man* (New York: Mentor Books, 1964), p. 1.

26. Google Books Library Project—an enhanced catalogue of the world's books. Available at: www.google.com/googlebooks/library.html.

Chapter 4

The World Wide Web as a Hypermedia System

Diagram of the Memex, *Life*, September 10, 1945, p. 123.

As suggested in the previous chapter, the Internet and the World Wide Web represent a further evolution of hypertext and hypermedia systems. They are in fact the realization of Bush's Memex. In developing the main thesis of this chapter, I will go beyond Bush's conception of the Memex as a research machine and universal library to further argue that the Internet and the World Wide Web are part of the larger phenomenon I term the "Difference Engine."

The Origins of the Internet and the World Wide Web

The Internet is an immediate product of the Cold War. Its origins can be traced back to the mid-1950s when the American military formed the Advanced Research Projects Agency (ARPA) in order to assure that the United States would not fall behind the Soviet Union in terms of science and technology. In 1962 theorists argued that it would be possible to connect computers together at different locations in networks that would allow them to communicate with one another using a common language. Seven years later in 1969 an experimental system known as ARPANET was put into operation, connecting computers at the University of California at Los Angeles, Stanford Research Institute and the University of Utah.

In 1972 the first Electronic Mail or E-mail program was created. It allowed messages to be sent and received across the network. In 1984, the number of computers on ARPANET reached over one thousand. These computer sites were located almost exclusively at research universities. In 1986 the National Science Foundation created the NSF Net backbone on ARPANET. Five super-computing centers were set around the United States that provided access to high-speed computing for users from across the country.

By 1987 over ten thousand computers were connected via ARPANET—mostly in university and research centers. In 1990, ARPANET as a government project ceased to exist when the network officially became known as the Internet. A year later in 1991, the first Internet search and navigation tools were created. In 1992, World Wide Web (WWW) technology, which provided the Internet with visual and graphic interface technology, was released. The World Wide Web also made it possible to hyperlink Internet sites. According to the U.S. Census Bureau, approximately 40% of the adult population in the United States had access to the Internet in the year 2000.[1] Estimates for 2009 saw this number increase to 74.1% of the population or a total of 227,719,000 users.[2] Estimated use in 2009 for a worldwide population of 6,767,805,208 was 1,733,993,741 or 25.6%.[3] With the growth of mobile computing devices with Internet connections, the World Wide Web is becoming more and more widespread in its use, becoming particularly important in less economically developed regions of the world—particularly in the form of mobile computing.

Bush's Conception of the Memex as Anticipating the

Internet and the World Wide Web and Its Search Tools

When I use the Internet and the World Wide Web—and more specifically a Web browser—it is clear to me that I am using a piece of software that fulfills many of the same functions as Bush's Memex.

The first World Wide Web browser was developed in the early 1990s by the National Center for Supercomputing at the University of Illinois. Known as Mosaic, it was originally given away for free. Its initial significance lay in the fact that its button bars and pull-down menus made it extremely easy to use, thus making the Internet much more accessible.

Mosaic, and its commercial version Netscape Navigator were much more than just simplified access tools for the Internet. They also incorporate through various connected tools and search engines, as well as editing programs, the essential elements of the Memex. This is also true of more recently developed web browsers including the Microsoft Corporation's Explorer.

Bush saw the Memex as a commercial device. Users would buy sources of data that were of interest to them and load them onto the machine. Most of the contents of the Memex would be purchased on microfilm. These could include "books of all sorts, pictures, current periodicals, newspapers." Business correspondence could be loaded onto the machine as well. An editing system would allow for "direct entry."[4] Unlike Bush's Memex, the Internet and World Wide Web have not depended just on commercial databases. The great majority of websites currently available are free and non-commercial. Other differences are significant as well. Data, rather than being stored on the user's machine, as was the case with the Memex, is networked across computer servers, making the storage of information global in location, scope and size.

By using a web browser to connect to the Web, virtually unlimited amounts of visual and text data become available to the user. Business information can be downloaded (stock prices, tax information and so on) and manipulated in spreadsheets and word processing programs available in your computer. In addition, with most web browsers it is possible to create and edit your own Web pages.

One of the remarkable features of any web browser is the fact that it connects from its main screen into a series of search engines and directories such as Google—something that is simply taken for granted by most users today. This and similar search engines and directories give the user access to the resources that reside on the World Wide Web. Once an item is called up from the Web, it is loaded onto the user's computer. Multiple documents can be loaded, allowing the user to move back and forth between different sources. Notes can be made by the user as he or she works across multiple documents. Bush described almost exactly the same function for the Memex. In the case of his user:

A special button transfers him immediately to the first page of the index. Any given book of his library can thus be called up and consulted with far greater facility then if it were taken from a shelf. As he has several projection positions, he can leave one item in position while he calls up another. He can add marginal notes and comments.[5]

Fundamental to Bush's conception of the Memex was that it works on an associative basis—much like the human mind. Thus "leaves of grass" are associated with pages from a book of poems by Walt Whitman, rather than just with a type of plant found on the front lawns of suburban homes. According to Bush, the human mind:

> operates by association. With one item in its grasp, it snaps instantly to the next that is suggested by the association of thoughts, in accordance with some intricate web of trails carried by the cells of the brain. It has other characteristics, of course; trails that are not frequently followed are prone to fade, items are not fully permanent, memory is transitory. Yet the speed of action, the intricacy of trails, the detail of mental pictures, is awe-inspiring beyond all else in nature.[6]

Hypertext and hypermedia systems by definition operate on an associative basis. This is also a key concept underlying the World Wide Web where associated ideas are connected together by means of hyperlinks. So too was this a fundamental element of Bush's Memex—the idea of "tying" together different items. As Bush explained, the idea of associative indexing with the Memex involved:

> a provision whereby any item may be caused at will to select immediately and automatically another. This is the essential feature of the Memex. The process of tying two items together is the important thing.[7]

The idea of automatic linking is yet one more concept that has been built into the structure of the Internet and the World Wide Web. Search engines go out and search the Internet for various types of information thus fulfilling Bush's expectation that the Memex would learn "to do clever things for us in the handling of the mass of data we insert in it. We particularly expect it to from its own experience and to refine its own trails."[8]

Among the most useful tools included as part of web browsing software, is the bookmark or "favorites" file in which one can store Web site addresses as they are discovered and used. In doing so, it is possible to create a trail of where you have been—not unlike the white pebbles left by Hansel in the fairy tale that allowed him to find his way home again with his sister. Once again this realizes a critical feature of the Memex. According to Bush, with the Memex: "When the user is building a trail, he names it, inserts the name in his code book, and taps it out on his keyboard."[9]

For Bush, the Memex becomes a tool with which the user could record the associations he or she had made and then easily recall them for later use. Bush creates a scenario in which this process is described in detail. In a conversation with a friend of his, a scholar, several years after he has recorded some useful information on his Memex, explains how people often resist technological innovations, despite their obvious and immediate benefits. The scholar remembers material he had taken notes on involving the use of the Turkish bow in warfare. According to Bush, using the Memex he has at the touch of his fingers:

> an example, in the fact that the outranged Europeans still failed to adopt the Turkish bow. In fact, he has a trail on it. A touch brings up the code book. Tapping a few keys projects the head of the trail. A lever runs through it at will, stopping at intersecting items, going off on side excursions. It is an interesting trail, pertinent to the discussion. So he sets a reproducer in action, photographs the whole trail out, and passes it to his friend for insertion in his own Memex, there to be linked into the more general trail.[10]

Illustration of the Memex in use, *Life,* **September 10, 1945, p. 124.**

It is now commonplace for people to share web addresses with one another by e-mailing them back and forth, or by exchanging them with a disk. From a functional point of view this is the same thing that is done when Bush's scholar gives the trail he has recorded on his Memex to his friend to insert into his own machine. Doing so, in many regards serves the same function as a scholar sharing a bibliography with a friend or colleague.

Implicit in the development of the Internet and World Wide Web is the creation of a new means of organizing and accessing materials, and new roles for the people who use it. This idea was also anticipated by Bush, who suggested that the invention of the Memex would lead to the creation of "a new profession of trail blazers, those who find delight in the task of establishing useful trails through the enormous mass of the common record. The inheritance from the master becomes not only his additions to the world's record, but for his disciples the entire scaffolding by which they were erected."[11]

The World Wide Web connected to a browser such as Microsoft Explorer is essentially Vannevar Bush's Memex. However, it also something much greater. To begin with, although Bush envisioned a machine with massive storage capacity, the Internet and the World Wide Web are far beyond what he had anticipated as being possible. In addition, Bush did not anticipate the extent to which his Memex system would be further modified by related computer technologies, nor did he adequately consider the cultural and social implications of what he was proposing—particularly in terms of Networked and Collective models of Intelligence.

Continental Contributions: The Work of Pierre Levy

Earlier we discussed the work of Douglas Engelbart and his ideas concerning Collective Intelligence. Englebart is not the only contemporary theorist concerned with the idea of Collective Intelligence. In France, Pierre Levy a professor of hypertext and hypermedia studies in the Department of Hypermedia, University of Paris-VIII has also contributed to the discussion of the emergence of a new model of "Collective Intelligence" that is a result of hypermedia and the Internet.

Levy provides what is perhaps the most reflective and thoughtful source to be found in the literature on the possibilities of Collective Intelligence. While widely followed in Europe, his work has only recently begun to be translated into English.[12] He argues that the computer revolution is part of a process of cultural evolution that is leading us "toward the creation of a new medium of communication, thought, and work."[13] Like Engelbart, he sees the computer as an intelligence enhancer, or as he terms it a "cognitive prothesis."[14] Even more important for Levy is the fact that the computer and the associated technologies of the Internet and World Wide Web make possible a shared or Collective Intelligence.

Levy's ideas about Collective Intelligence go beyond those of Engelbart in their emphasis on social, economic and political issues. For Levy, "The prosperity of a nation, geographical region, business, or individual depends upon their ability to navigate the knowledge space."[15] For Levy, the *knoweldge space* that is being created by the computerization of society and the realization of the

Difference Engine will almost certainly "take precedence over the spaces of earth, territory and commerce that preceded it."[16]

This is true of all aspects of the educational system (but particularly higher education), as it is of society, economics and politics in general. In *Collective Intelligence* he attempts to map the new knowledge space that is coming into being. For Levy this new knowledge space is realized through the creation of a "collective intelligence." According to him, by means of the computerization of society, and the mechanism of what I call the Difference Engine, we have the potential to "promote the construction of intelligent communities in which our social and cognitive potential can be mutually enhanced and developed."[17] Technologies such as the Internet and the World Wide Web "will serve to filter and help us navigate knowledge, and enable us to think collectively rather than simply haul masses of information about with us."[18]

The Creation of the Cosmopedia

Levy names the new knowledge space that is a result of the emergence of collective intelligence the *cosmopedia*. Going beyond the static text of the printed word and traditional encyclopedia, the *cosmopedia* combines "static images, video, sound, interactice simulation, interactive maps, expert systems, dynamic ideographs, virtual reality, artificial life, etc."[19]

According to Levy, the *cosmopedia* breaks down the artifical boundaries between the disciplines, making knowledge "a large patchwork" in which almost any field can be folded into another. Essentially Levy argues that the power of disciplinary knowledge is challenged through the creation of a new rhetorical space provided by the computer.

Levy believes that the network culture of the *cosmopedia* "has not yet stabilized," and that its technical infrastructure is still in formation.[20] We are faced with fundamental political and cultural choices. Our means of communicating, collaborating and reproducing knowledge are rapidly changing. Perhaps the only precedent for this type of change—particularly as it confronts higher education—is the type of change that took place after the invention of movable type.   I t should be no surprise that we have had an extensive debate in recent years at all levels of the educational system as to what we should teach and what constitutes an education, or an educated person. For Levy, part of the reason for this debate lies in the revolutions taking place in communications and computers. According to Levy, we have become "nomads." According to him:

> Movement no longer means traveling from point to point on the surface of the globe, but crossing universes of problems, lived worlds, landscapes of meaning. These wan-derings among the textures of humanity may intersect the well-delineated paths of the circuits of communication and transport, but the heterogeneous navigations of the new nomads will investigate a different space.[21]

Levy argues that we are on very new cultural ground. That the new computer and telecommunication technologies are "transforming our intellectual capabilities as clearly as the mutations of our genetic heritage."[22] We are seeing a rapid modification of our environment—both intellectual and social. While mankind is not threatened by extinction, he believes that it is essential that we engage in a form of collective intelligence—one made possible by our technologies. In doing so,

> we will gradually create the technologies, sign systems, forms of social organization and regulation that enable us to think as a group, concentrate our intellectual and spiritual forces, and negotiate practical real-time solutions to the complex problems we must inevitably confront.[23]

*   *   *

The Internet and World Wide Web combined with Collective Intelligence and the Cosmopedia becomes yet another element of the Difference Engine. Other elements add to the construction of the system as well. In the following chapter we look first at simulation technologies, and then at the role of technologies of surveillance and control, and how each redefines the meaning of knowledge and literacy.

References

1. *Statistical Abstract of the United States, 2000* (Washington, DC: U.S. Government Printing Office), p. 568.
2. Internet World Stats. United States of America, Internet Usage. Available online at: www.internetworldstats.com/am/us.htm.
3. *Ibid.* World Internet Users and Populations Stats. Available online at: ww.internetworldstats.com/america.htm.
4. Greif, Irene, *Computer-Supported Cooperative Work: A Book of Readings* (California: Morgan Kaufmann Publishers, Inc., 1988), p. 30.
5. *Ibid*, p. 30.
6. *Ibid*, p. 29.
7. *Ibid*, p. 31.
8. Norman Meyrowitz, "Does it Reduce Cholesteral, Too?" in James M. Nyce and Paul Kahn, editors, *From Memex to Hypertext: Vannevar Bush and the Mind's Machine* (New York: Academic Press, 1991), p. 297.
9. *Greif*, p. 31.
10. *Ibid*, p. 32.
11. *Ibid*, p. 32.
12. Pierre Lévy, *Collective Intelligence: Mankind's Emerging World in Cyberspace*, translated by Robert Bononno with a Foreword by Eugene F. Provenzo Jr. (New York: Plenum Books, 1998). My discussion of Levy is losely based around my foreword to his book.
13. *Ibid*, p. 1.
14. *Ibid*, p. 5.
15. *Ibid*, p. 10.
16. *Ibid*, p. 13.
17. *Ibid*, p. 17.
18. *Ibid.*
19. *Ibid*, pp. 174-175. Also see Michel Authier and Pierre Levy, "La Cosmopédie, une utopie hypervisuelle," in *Culture technique*, 24 (April 1992): pp. 236-244.
20. *Ibid*, p. xxi.
21. *Ibid*, p. xxii-xxiii.
22. *Ibid*, p. xiii.
23. *Ibid*, p. xxvii.

Chapter 5

Cyberspace, Hyperreality, and the Culture of Simulation

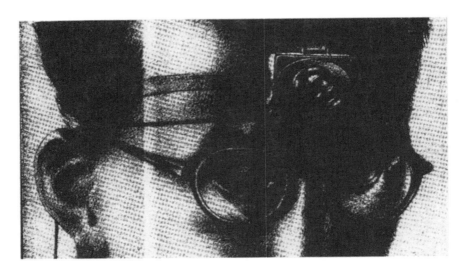

A Cyclops Camera using a universal-focus lens allows the user to record any information or data one wishes (*Life*, September 10, 1945, p. 112). As a device it anticipates the idea of wiring humans into computers.

In a prophetic report dealing with the computerization of society first published for the French government in 1978, Simon Nora and Alain Minc argued that the computer revolution was not only the most important technological innovation of recent years, but that it was the one that constituted "the common factor that speeds the development of all the others."[1]

As we enter the new millennium, it seems clear that Nora and Minc were not quite right. The computer does not simply speed other technological developments, but instead defines them. One can see this, for example, in the case of television. A decade ago a television was a television. Today it is as much a computer as a TV. What was a television has been transformed into a computer. In a similar way, fashion the networked computer takes the technology of the radio and the phonograph player and merges them together in the iPod or digital music player—making it possible to "broadcast" on demand on the Internet and World Wide Web sound recordings.

Some changes are not as complete, but nonetheless are profound in their own right. My car has approximately thirty computers of different types (microchips) that regulate its breaks, control its fuel consumption, and record the time on a digital clock. It is still visibly a car with four wheels and windshield wipers, but it is also many computers working as part of a carefully coordinated networked system.

The transformation of cars and radios and televisions are all physical manifestations of the "Difference Engine" and the increasing role it plays in our lives. Yet the Difference Engine is more than just its physical manifestations. It is also its metaphors and the models of the world it constructs for us.

In the following chapter we begin to explore these newly emerging models by looking at two closely related phenomenon: 1. cyberspace and 2. hyperreality and simulation.

Cyberspace

In his 1984 science fiction novel *Neuromancer*, William Gibson first coined the term *cyberspace*. In *Neuromancer*, and in subsequent works such as *Count Zero* and *Mona Lisa Overdrive*, Gibson describes a not too distant future in which the world is dominated by powerful multinational corporations. Urban life has collapsed; cosmetic surgery and reconstruction are the norm, along with neural implants and Artificial Intelligences who literally take on lives of their own.

Gibson's fictional world is tied together by an electronic construct called the "matrix." This is a vast electronic network that connects together all of the world's computers and information systems. Its primitive origins are found in video games and early computer experiments conducted by the military, as well as in the Internet.

In order to navigate through the massive electronic database of the matrix, users are connected, or interfaced, through electrodes wired to their brains. The graphic representations the user sees in order to navigate through the matrix, or simulation, is called cyberspace.

Gibson describes cyberspace as:

> A consensual hallucination experienced by billions of legitimate operators in every nation, by children being taught mathematical concepts . . . A graphic representation of data abstracted from the banks of every computer in the human system. Unthinkable complexity. Lines of light ranged in the nonspace of the mind, clusters and constellations of datas. Like city lights, receding.[2]

Michael Benedikt, a professor of architecture and design at the University of Texas, has described cyberspace as:

> A new universe, a parallel universe created and sustained by the world's computers and communication lines. A world in which the global traffic of knowledge, secrets, measurements, indicators, entertainments, and alter-human agency takes on form: sights, sounds, presences never seen on the surface of the earth blossoming in a vast electronic night.[3]

Cyberspace exists, according to Benedikt, "wherever electricity runs."[4] It is a realm of "pure information," a "soft hail of electrons."[5] It is also a place which Benedikt argues—for the most part—does not yet exist. It is more a fantasy or desire than a reality.[6]

Why then does the term cyberspace dominate so many current conversations involving computers and culture? Gibson provides an explanation in explaining how he invented the word:

> Assembled the word cyberspace from small and readily available components of language. Neologic spasm; the primal act of pop poetics. Preceded any concept whatever. Slick and hollow—awaiting received meaning. All I did: folded words as taught. Now other words accrete in the interstices.[7]

Cyberspace is a word that describes the new world that is beginning to be realized from an information point of view. It is a word describing the post-modern or post-typographic condition. Cyberspace, at the broadest conceptual level, is the global village, the Internet, the Information Super Highway. It is humanity connected by electronic information and the hyperlinks of the World Wide Web.

Cyberspace is also a much narrower literary construct and metaphor. At its most basic level within novels like *Neuromancer*, it is a mnemonic device—a visual construct of the world of electrons and information that flows around us, but which we cannot see or directly experience.

In this context, cyberspace is a simulation. It imitates the real and extends its meaning through the creation of hyperrealities. To a remarkable degree, contemporary culture, computing and the "Difference Engine" are rooted in simulations or hyperrealities like cyberspace.

Computing and the Culture of Simulation

At the beginning of this book, I introduced the work of the French social theorist Jean Baudrillard. Baudrillard, along with other theorists such as the Italian semiotician and novelist Umberto Eco, argues that we are increasingly creating a world in which the real is substituted for the hyperreal—in which the simulation is understood to be authentic.

This occurs in many different ways. Television and its depiction of the family as part of situation comedies is a simulation of real life. Epcot Center at Disney World, with its recreations of Venice, Norway and China, simulates the real world. Advertisements with airbrushed photographs of models and commercial products are simulations. When we watch a movie or play a computer game, we are entering into a simulated culture or hyperreality.

Simulation is by no means a new phenomenon in Western culture. The development of modern painting and book illustration during the Renaissance represents examples of attempts to substitute the real with simulations or models. Perspective drawing, in many regards, is nothing more than an attempt to substitute a drawing for that which we perceive naturally in the real world.

The area of computer simulation that has received greatest attention in recent years is Virtual Reality. Virtual Reality is, in a certain sense, the ultimate hypermedia extension. At its most sophisticated level it involves putting on "computer clothing," which includes devices such as eye-phones (a tiny pair of video screens that are mounted in front of each eye to provide stereo vision of a computer-created reality), data gloves (in which sensors lining one's hand communicate movement to a graphics computer), and stereo earphones and positional sensing equipment in order to enter a simulated computer environment.[8]

Simpler systems such as Ninetendo's hugely popular Wii video game console use a handheld pointing device and detect motion in three dimensions. As of the end of 2009 a total of over 67 million Wii units had been shipped.[9] Using the Wii sport programs and simulations make it possible to experience something that is like skateboarding or skiing down a mountain, playing professional football or skydiving. As "sense around" systems are developed, it becomes possible to create something approaching Aldous Huxley's "feelies."

As such systems become increasingly available, will a generation of virtual reality "couch potatoes" play football on the video screen rather than on the football field? We believe that this is already happening. One need only look at the extraordinary popularity of video game systems such as the Wii and Microsoft's Xbox to see the extent to which this is the case.

The potential for the machine to dehumanize as it augments our experience as part of cyber or hyperspace simulations is enormous. Yet in raising these issues, I do not wish to appear to be rejecting the technology or its potential. We have used tools to create imaginary worlds or simulations throughout our history. Novels such as Jules Verne's *Twenty Thousand Leagues Under the Sea* are on one level a simulation, as are great film classics as diverse as *Citizen Kane* or *Star Wars*.

The integration of virtual reality and hypermedia simulations has enormous potential. A project of the author's, for example, involves the recreation of the *Exhibit of the American Negroes* that was part of the Paris 1900 Exposition. The project, makes it possible to visit a hypertext/hypermedia reconstruction of the exhibit, which was assembled under the direction of the African-American sociologist W.E.B. DuBois, and was a grand prizewinner in the Social Science Division at the Exposition. It included thousands of photographs of black life and culture at the turn of the century, as well as examples of hundreds of books and pamphlets written by African-American authors that had been sent to Paris for exhibit by the Library of Congress.

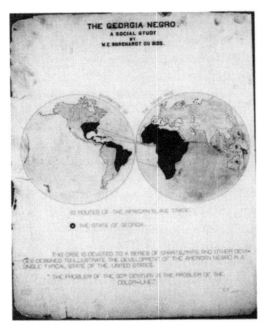

Title Page from the Georgia Negro Exhibit, part of the Exhibit of American Negroes, Paris 1900 World's Fair.

The project is available as a CD-ROM and an Internet site, as well as a forthcoming book. It uses a very simple walk-through interface system that allows the user to "click" on different parts of the exhibit and "pull up" different types of information (photos, books, reports and so on).

"Clickable" or "hot spot" hypermedia map for the web site The Exhibit of the American Negro, Exposition Universelle, Paris 1900 (http://129.171.53.1/ep/Paris/home.htm), created by the author.

Programs like this are nothing new. Their origins are in the computer mapping projects such as the *Aspen Project*, which Nicholas Negroponte and his colleagues undertook in the late 1970s, in which a film was made of the different streets of Aspen, Colorado, and then programmed into a computer. The program allowed the user to drive through a simulated version of the town, stopping wherever the user wanted.

Programs like this can incorporate extensive hypertext and hypermedia functions, and have been in widespread use since the early 1990s. The pioneering hypermedia program *A Passion for Art: Renoir, Cezanne, Matisse and Dr. Barnes*, for example, provides a personal gallery tour through the country's greatest private collection of post-impressionist art—the A. S. Barnes collection. Essentially, *A Passion for Art* is a hypermedia database and virtual museum that provides the user with a complete visual and text catalogue of the paintings included in the A. S. Barnes collection.[10]

Using the *Passion for Art* hypermedia program, the user can take a "virtual" tour of the museum and its holdings. Not only can you walk through the individual galleries of the museum, but historical timelines can be consulted, as well as archives including information on major paintings included in the Barnes Collection.

While an extraordinary data source is made available to the user of *A Passion for Art*, the program is limited in that it is but a simulation of the museum, its paintings and its archives. Cyberspace and online hypermedia museums like the *Passion for Art* program are rapidly coming into existence in many different formats. One need only go on the Internet and the World Wide Web to see the extent to which this is the case. Sites such as the Louvre in Paris (www.paris.org/Musees/Louvre/), the Metropolitan Museum of Art in New York City (www.metmuseum.org/), the Smithsonian Institution in Washington, D.C. (http://www.si.edu/search/sisearch.htm) and the Victoria and Albert Museum in London (www.vam.ac.uk/) are examples of museum sites with gallery tours and access to archival and research materials that are located on the World Wide Web.

Programs such as *Second Life* make it possible for users to explore a simulated three-dimensional space and interact with others by means of an avatar, a 3-D representation of oneself. Users called "Residents" can explore virtual spaces through their avatars, create and sell virtual property, and interact with others residents.

Second Life provide a means by which to understand the direction that computer simulations are taking us, simulations of the type predicted by Gibson and Bendikt cited earlier in this chapter. It is entirely conceivable to imagine people who in the near future will lead the greater part of their recreational and working lives inside of some form of cyberspace. This scenario is described in Neal Stephenson's novel *Snowcrash*, where the story's main character Hiro delivers pizzas during the day, and at night takes on the role of a freelance hacker and samurai in a computer simulation known as the "metaverse." In the real world he is an obscure figure living at the edge of society. In his "second life" in the metaverse he is a man of influence and is wealthy in terms of virtual property.[11]

The Promise and Peril of Simulations

The use of Virtual Reality combined with hypertext and hypermedia programs make it possible for a paraplegic to enter a virtual simulation and experience things at a level that otherwise would not be possible. Imagine, for a moment, being almost totally paralyzed, but suddenly able to participate in an intimate physical relationship (albeit it a computer-mediated one) with another normal or physically challenged individual. Imagine being able to walk through the Swiss Alps, experience diving under the ocean or playing a game such as soccer or tennis. Of course the question remains, is the simulation "genuine" when compared with the actual experience?

The implications of hypermedia and virtual reality for education are potentially enormous. Students learning mathematics, for example, no longer need to work from just equations and formulas, but can see visual representations of what they are studying. To a large extent this is already happening with programs like Maple, Mathematica and Theorist.[12]

The use of these technologies, however, also changes the nature of teaching and learning and the cultural and educational environment of the classroom. In Chapter 1 of this work, I referred to C. A. Bowers's *The Cultural Dimensions of Educational Computing*. In that work, Bowers establishes a powerful argument for the non-neutrality of the computer—one which is profoundly important for educators to understand. According to him:

> Understanding how the educational use of computers influences our pattern of thinking, and thus contributes to changes in the symbolic underpinnings of the culture, should be considered an essential aspect of computer literacy.[13]

Bowers's arguments are not only true in an educational context, but in the larger cultural context as well. How does hypertext and hypermedia, and simulation and hyperreality, redefine our ways of thinking and organizing the.world.[14] What models of culture are created or implied through the use of hypertext and hypermedia systems? Through the culture of simulation? What cultural patterns are strengthened or weakened through their use? Are their ideologies inherent in their design? Who benefits from their use? What delivery systems are used and how do they channel or focus what is learned? We can begin to answer questions such as these by looking at some of the recently developed simulation games that employ hypermedia and simulation models such as the classic computer game Populous.

Populous as a Model of Culture

Hypertext and hypermedia systems, if open-ended, imply that knowledge is fluid and essentially interdisciplinary in nature. Individuals using such systems should not only be able to see the historical links between ideas, but also come to understand the importance of analogous thinking in the creation of new knowledge. Students using hypertext and hypermedia systems, for example, should be able to learn that many texts and interpretations are often subject to revision.

In this context, a classic computer game like Populous can provide us with insight into hypermedia systems as simulations and into the limitations inherent in such models.[15] In Populous, you assume the role of one of two gods who rule a world and its people. One of the gods is evil and the other is good. Each god is assigned a population of people whom they nurture and try to help flourish. As a review of the game explains: "Your task is to make the lives of your people as prosperous as possible, fostering their growth by divinely manipulating their environment."[16]

Any simulation represents a specific point of view. The perspective provided in Populous is of an omniscient god who shapes and directs the lives of the people (called "walkers") on the planet. A review of the game by Matthew Firme explains how:

> Skeptics will be surprised at how enjoyable playing a god turns out to be. The walkers, both good and bad, are fascinating to watch as they move about. They really seem to have lives of their own, and your control over their lives gives you an undeniable sense of power. . . . Soon you'll find yourself feeling parental about your followers, nurturing them and watching them grow. You'll be happy to wipe out the evil walkers with volcanoes, swamps and earthquakes should they stand in the way of your chosen people.[17]

What is clearly at work in this simulation are a series of assumptions about the desirability of power and control, and about the need of other people to be directed. The viewpoint is that of an all-powerful god who acts on people (walkers) rather than with people (walkers). The world is shaped and defined by a relatively narrow and circumscribed set of forces (volcanoes, earthquakes and so on).

A simulation such as Populous is neither neutral, nor without a specific point of view. As Firme notes: "It's amazingly easy to develop delusions of grandeur while playing Populous,...."[18] Will children playing games such as Populous simply assume that this is how the world is run? Will they incorporate such models into their own lives? Does a teacher using such a system in the classroom have any means by which to distinguish good from evil, to delineate variables that may be affecting what is occurring in the simulation? How does the omniscient perspective influence what the players do? Would they act differently if they were one of the walkers?

Concerns about the use of a simulation such as *Populous* directly address Bowers's question of "whether the current state of computer technology used in the classroom strengthens those cultural orientations contributing to a technicist social order and weakens others that cannot be integrated into the new emerging order."[19] In the end, it is clear that the use of simulations is neither neutral, nor problem free. It should also be noted that as increasingly sophisticated simulations are created using technologies such as virtual reality, the power of these simulations over the user has the potential to become even greater.

Living with Simulation and the Hyperreality

Part of the post-modern condition is that we are surrounded by the simulated and hyperreal. The "Difference Engine" in its related parts contributes to a culture of simulation, where the model of things increasingly takes the place of the reality. I believe that this condition increasingly leads us away from our human selves.

In *Beyond the Gutenberg Galaxy*,[20] I made reference to the work of Ernest Becker and the image of humanity as either machine (*l'homme machine*) or as meaning seekers and meaning makers (*homo poeta*). Like Becker, I argued that we create evil when we design structures or institutions that make it impossible for us to act productively and creatively.[21] Virtual reality and hypertext simulations have the potential to greatly expand our creativity and imagination and our understanding of the world. These systems, however, based as they are on computers, are not neutral and must be understood in terms of their capacity to shape and direct us.

In the Victorian utopian novel *Erewhon*, Samuel Butler describes a country called Erewhon ("nowhere" approximately spelled backwards) in which all machines have been destroyed because it is felt that machines had begun to develop more rapidly than humans. In "The Book of the Machines," the most sacred of all of the texts in Erewhon, the anonymous author explains that: "Whenever precision is required man flies to the machine at once," but:

> How many men at this hour are living in a state of bondage to the machines? How many spend their whole lives from cradle to the grave, in tending them by night and by day? Is it not clear that the machines are gaining ground upon us, when we reflect upon the increasing number of those who are bound down to them as slaves, and of those who devote their whole souls to the advancement of the mechanical kingdom.[22]

Butler feared that human intelligence would be superseded by machine intelligence. In novels such as Frank Herbert's *Dune*, computers are banned from society as a result of their tendency to usurp the process of human decision-making.[23]

While I believe in the potential of computers to augment our intellect and understanding of the world, I am convinced that we must approach them with a much greater critical awareness of how they function than has been the case up until this time. Joseph Weizenbaum has astutely pointed to the fact that men bind themselves to the machines that they use—that they become physical and psychological extensions of the self. For man (humankind), machines such as computers:

> become literally part of him and modify him, and thus alter the basis of his affective relationship to himself. One would expect man to cathect more intensely to instruments that couple directly to his own intellectual, cognitive, and emotive functions than to machines that merely extend the power of his muscles.[24]

Computers and technologies such as hypertext and hypermedia are neither neutral, nor without consequences in their use. Simulations construct very specific models of the world—ones that include their own values and ideologies. To repeat Bowers's argument one more time—the computer, and in turn the "Difference Engine," is not a neutral technology.

E. M. Forster—"The Machine Stops"

The non-neutrality of the computer, and its potential to shape and redefine us from a cultural and social perspective, is described in E. M. Forster's 1923 short story "The Machine Stops." In this work a woman is living in:

> a small room, hexagonal in shape, like the cell of a bee. It is lighted neither by window nor by lamp, yet it is filled with a soft radiance. There are no apertures for ventilation, yet the air is fresh. There are no musical instruments, and yet . . . . . this room is throbbing with melodious sounds.[25]

The room is part of a great network of worldwide machines that connects virtually everyone. It anticipates the possibilities of a worldwide hypertext network much like that currently found on the Internet and World Wide Web, or a network system of the type proposed decades ago by Ted Nelson in his book *Literary Machines*.[26]

The woman's name is Vashti. One day her son Kuno contacts her on the "Machine." Speaking to her through the machine from a location far off in another part of the world, he explains to her that the Machine is a human creation and necessarily limited:

> Men made it, do not forget that. Great men, but men. The Machine is much, but it is not everything. I see something like you in this plate, but I do not see you. I hear something like you in this plate, but I do not see you. I hear something through this telephone, but I do not hear you.[27]

In the above passages Kuno raises what is a fundamental question about the use of hypertext, hypermedia and virtual reality systems. Through their use do we come to construct a distorted and diminished reality?

Vashti, for example, after disconnecting her contact with her son, wondered whether or not he looked sad. She could not be sure for the Machine did not transmit *nuances* of expression. It only gave a general idea of people—an idea that was good enough for all practical purposes, Vashti thought. The imponderable bloom, declared by a discredited philosophy to be the actual essence of intercourse, was rightly ignored by the Machine, just as the imponderable bloom of the grape was ignored by the manufacturers of artificial fruit. Something "good enough" had long since been accepted by our race.[28]

Will hypermedia and virtual reality lead us into accepting simulations as substitutes for the real thing. Forster's character Vashti addresses the question by reflecting on:

the civilization that had immediately preceded her own—the civilization that had mistaken the functions of the system, and had used it for bringing people to things, instead of for bringing things to people! Those funny old days, when men went for change of air instead of changing the air in the rooms![29]

Paralleling the type of fears raised by Samuel Butler in "The Book of Machines" in *Erewhon*, Kuno explains to his mother that:

We created the Machine to do our will, but we cannot make it do our will now. It has robbed us of the sense of space and of the sense of touch, it has blurred every human relation and narrowed down love to a carnal act, it has paralyzed our bodies and our ills, and now it compels us to worship it. The Machine develops—but not on our lines. The Machine proceeds—but not to our goal. We only exist as the blood corpuscles that course through its arteries, and if it could work without us it would let us die.[30]

According to Kuno:

Those who still wanted to know what the earth was like had after all only to listen to some gramophone, or to look into some cinematophobe. And even the lecturers acquiesced when they found that a lecture on the sea was none the less stimulating when compiled out of other lectures that had already been delivered on the same subject. "Beware of first-hand ideas!" exclaimed one of the most advanced of them. "First-hand ideas do not really exist. They are but the physical impressions produced by love and fear, and on this gross foundation who could erect a philosophy? Let your ideas be second-hand, and if possible tenth-hand, for then they will be removed from the disturbing element—direct observation.[31]

In doing so, according to Kuno:

> there will come a generation that has got beyond facts, beyond impressions, a generation absolutely colourless, a generation 'seraphically free from taint of personality,' which will see the French Revolution not as it happened, nor as they would like it to have happened, but as it would have happened, had it taken place in the days of the Machine.[32]

Forster's "The Machine Stops" is a cautionary tale. It suggests a world that may likely come into being in one form or another if we do not attempt to really understand the potential limitations of hypertext, hypermedia and virtual reality systems. Forster's story makes me wonder about what is happening to people like myself who spend much of their time staring at computer screens, communicating with others via e-mail and avoiding the library when they can use online services instead.

*   *   *

Clearly hypertext and hypermedia, the Internet and the World Wide Web and simulations, whether in the form of games or metaverses, represent important emerging elements of the "Difference Engine." Each represent specific ways of looking at, interpreting and acting in the world. While each has the potential to augment our intelligence and understanding of the world around us, each also can limit and circumscribe our humanity. In the following chapter, we will look in more detail at the computer and the problem of control, and how control and surveillance functions constitute a major element of the Difference Engine.

Notes

1. Simon Nora and Alain Minc, *The Computerization of Society: A Report to the President of France* (Cambridge: MIT Press, 1980), p. 3.
2. William Gibson, *Neuromancer* (New York: Ace Books, 1984), p. 51.
3. Michael Benedikt, *Cyberspace: First Steps* (Cambridge: MIT Press, 1992), p. 1.
4. *Ibid*, p. 2.
5. *Ibid*, p. 3.
6. *Ibid*.
7. William Gibson, "Academy Leader," in *Benedikt*, p. 27.
8. Steven Levy, "Brave New World," *Rolling Stone*, June 14, 1990, p. 92.
9. "Wii," *Wikipedia* article available online at: http://en.wikipedia.org/wiki/Wii.
10. A completely revised version of this program, which was first released in 1994, was reissued by the Barnes Foundation in October of 2003. In the revised version the works of art are at detailed, 1024 x 768 resolution and in millions of colors, and the audio commentary and music are in stereo. The updated version of the program provides a remarkably good example of the potential of a virtual museum tour.

    Examples of virtual museum tours and exhibits available online include: The Warhol, Carnegie Museums of Pittsburgh (http://www.warhol.org/); The Metropolitan Museum of Art (www.metmuseum.org/special/index.asp); Virtual Tour of the National Gallery, Smithsonian Institution (www.nga.gov/collection/); Tour of the National Women's History Museum (www.nmwh.org/home/selfguidedtour.htm); Field Museum of Natural History (www.fieldmuseum.org/exhibits/online_exhib. htm); and National Museum of Woman and the Arts (www.nmwa.org/).
11. Neal Stephenson, *Snow Crash* (New York: Bantam Books, 1992).
12. See James Paul Gee's *What Video Games Have to Teach Us About Learning and Literacy* (New York: Palgrave Macmillan, 2003), for what new computer technologies have to tell us about teaching and learning.
13. C. A. Bowers, *The Cultural Dimensions of Educational Computing* (New York: Teachers College Press, 1988), p. 3.
14. *Ibid*.
15. Almost exactly the same arguments can be made using the game series *The Sims*.
16. Matthew A. Firme, "Populous," *Game Player's PC Strategy Guide*, March/April 1990, p. 91.
17. *Ibid*.
18. *Ibid.*, p. 90.
19. Bowers, *The Cultural Dimensions of Educational Computing*, p. 6.
20. Eugene F. Provenzo Jr., *Beyond the Gutenberg Galaxy: Microcomputers and the Emergence of Post-Typographic Culture* (New York: Teachers College Press, 1986), p. 72.
21. Ernest Becker, *The Structure of Evil* (New York: Free Press, 1978), pp. 169–174.
22. Samuel Butler, *Erewhon* (New York: Airmont, 1967), p. 150.
23. Frank Herbert, *Dune* (New York: Berkley Medallion Books, 1965).
24. Joseph Weizenbaum, *Computer Power and Human Reason,* (San Francisco: W. H. Freeman and Company, 1976), p. 9.
25. E. M. Forster, "The Machine Stops" included in *The Collected Tales of E. M. Forster* (New York: Alfred A. Knopf, 1959), p. 144.

26. Theodor Nelson, *Literary Machines* (Theodor Nelson, Edition 87.1, 1987).
27. *Ibid*, pp. 146–147.
28. *Ibid*, p. 148.
29. *Ibid*, p. 153.
30. *Ibid*, p. 176.
31. *Ibid*, p. 183.
32. *Ibid*.

Chapter 6

Computing and the Panoptic Sort

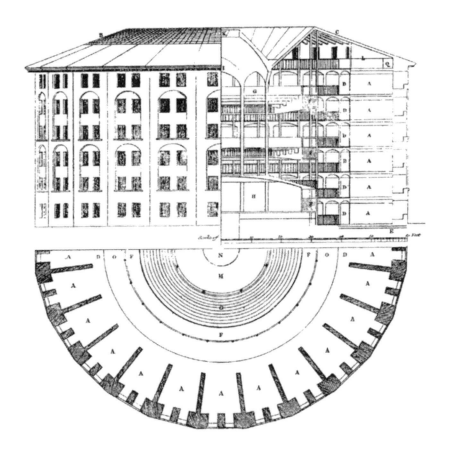

Plan for Jeremy Bentham's Panopticon from John Bowring, editor, *The Works of Jeremy Bentham*, vol. iv, 1843.

Perhaps the most disturbing vision of social control to be found in literature is that described by George Orwell in his novel 1984.[1] In the novel, Big Brother keeps the population of Oceania under continual observation through the use of a system of two-way televisions or "telescreens." Located at a central point in each citizen's home, the telescreen could be dimmed, but never turned completely off. It "received and transmitted simultaneously." Any sound—even at the level of a low whisper would be detected. One was never able to leave its field of vision. There was "no way of knowing whether you were being watched at any given moment. . . every movement scrutinized."[2]

In Oceania, posters showing Big Brother, inscribed with "Big Brother is Watching," looked down from every stairwell, from every street corner, and from somewhere in every public place. The visual image of Big Brother was "so contrived that the eyes follow you about when you move."

Significantly, Orwell did not include computers in his anti-utopia— there being no indication in his work that he anticipated them as a future technology. Yet the mechanisms for carrying out the functions of control, censorship and indoctrination described by him are implicit in contemporary networked computer systems. Using currently available computer technology, it is possible to establish systems of continuous surveillance and control like those found in Orwell's novel.[3]

In the following chapter, I examine the implications of current computer technology for intellectual and personal freedom in our society, and for the education of our children. Implicit in the arguments of this chapter is the conviction that the non-neutral computer, as Marshall McLuhan and C. A. Bowers argue, "frames" how we think and act.[4]

We are faced, in a post-typographic and networked culture, with a new type of electronic literacy that is subject to greater control and manipulation than was the case in the typographic culture of books and print. Literacy in a post-typographic culture involves being "connected." As a result, the data sources from which we draw our information can also be used to track and in turn manipulate and control us.

Critical to understanding the potential for control in networked computer systems is the work of the French social historian Michel Foucault.

Michel Foucault and the Power of Normalization

In Discipline and Punish Foucault was concerned with the emergence of modern forms of social regulation and control. These new models brought with them the exercise of a new type of power—the power of normalization. Normalizing power—which in the eighteenth century manifested itself in penal institutions, hospitals, factories and schools—has come to be realized in our own era through instrumentalities provided initially by mainframe computers and in turn by networked computer systems. According to Foucault, by the end of the eighteenth century a shift had occurred away from focusing on the power of individual men (monarchial power)—a reversal of the "axis of individualization"—toward the collection of records and information about individuals over whom power could be exercised. For Foucault, knowledge and power directly imply one another:

> there is no power relation without the correlative constitution of a field of knowledge, nor any knowledge that does not presuppose and constitute at the same time power relations.[5]

According to Foucault, the English utilitarian philosopher Jeremy Bentham (1748-1832) was the social theorist from the period who most completely understood the emergence of the new models of knowledge/power and social control. In particular, Bentham's *Panopticon; or the Inspection House* outlined a master plan for the observation and control of individuals living and working in any of a number of institutions, including: "prisons, houses of industry, work-houses, poor-houses, manufactories, mad-houses, lazarettos, hospitals and schools."[6]

The main element in Bentham's plan was a penitentiary inspection-house, which he called a "Panopticon." As he described it:

The building is circular.

The apartments of the prisoners occupy the circumference. You may call them, if you please the *cells*.

These *cells* are divided from one another, and the prisoners by that means secluded from all communication with each other, by *partitions* in the form of *radii* issuing from the circumference towards the centre, and extending as many feet as shall be thought necessary to form the largest dimension of the cell.

The apartment of the inspector occupies the centre; you may call it if you please the *inspector's lodge*.[7]

The inspector's lodge had numerous windows that made it possible to peer into the prisoners' cells. Lighting was arranged in such a way that the inspector in the central lodge or tower of the Panopticon could keep the prisoners in their individual cells under constant observation without them being aware that they were being observed. Speaking tubes connected the inspector with the prisoners. The slightest whisper of a prisoner could be heard by the inspector in his central tower.

According to Foucault, Bentham's plan for the Panopticon reversed the principle of the dungeon, which enclosed and hid the prisoner, depriving him of light. Instead, through an ingenious use of architecture, the Panopticon enclosed and held the prisoner in what Foucault refers to as a constant trap of visibility.[8] As he explains, the prisoner:

> is seen, but he does not see; he is the object of information, never a subject in communication. The arrangement of his room, opposite the central tower, imposes on him an axial visibility; but the divisions of the ring, those separated cells, imply a lateral invisibility. And this invisibility is a guarantee of order. If the inmates are convicts, there is no danger of a plot, an attempt at collective escape, the planning of new crimes for the future, bad reciprocal influences; if they are patients, there is no danger of contagion; if they are madmen there is no risk of their committing violence upon one another; if they are schoolchildren, there is no copying, no noise, no chatter, no waste of time.[9]

Under Bentham's panoptic system, the individual came to believe that he was under constant observation. As long as the prisoner, or inmate, or student, sensed the possibility that he was being observed, the automatic functioning of power/knowledge and control was assured.

Computers as Contributing to the Potential for Control

C. A. Bowers has pointed out that the use of computers has increased the power of people "who have access to data, while leaving many others vulnerable to an increasing degree of technological surveillance."[10] There is clearly this potential with the use of hypertext and hypermedia systems and networked computer systems Using hypermedia systems that can network and "link" different databases and sources of information, it is possible to systematically monitor "consumer choices, political behavior, educational experiences, and work place productivity—as well as the nature of nearly all interactions of a citizen with a public or private institution."[11]

With the establishment of integrated or linked data sets (credit card records, insurance information, purchase patterns, etc.)—information is increasingly isolated and the potential for microsurveillance and control increased. The outcome is not as certain technological optimists have maintained, either positive or neutral. Bowers, for example, cites John Naisbet, the author of the bestseller *Megatrends*, to the effect that: "The new power is not money in the hands of the few, but information in the hands of the many."[12] Bowers argues, as I do, that such an interpretation is naive. A more likely model is based on the observation and control principles outlined by Foucault in reference to the work of Jeremy Bentham.

Many examples can be used to demonstrate this point—some of the most revealing come from relatively mundane sources. Various types of micro-surveillance have been in use for nearly two decades and have come into widespread use. A product called *Close-Up/LAN*, for example, was first introduced through Norton-Lambert Company in Santa Barbara, California during the late 1980s. In one of its early advertisements for product the following scenario for "helping people" is included:

> You're sitting at your PC on the 3rd floor working on a spreadsheet budget. Suddenly a message appears on your screen: "Bob requests help." You press a hot key, and like magic you are looking at Bob's screen. Without moving an inch you see that Bob is working on the company database. A dialog window appears and Bob explains his problem. Since your keyboard is active you instantly solve the problem, on Bob's computer. . . . With another hot key you decide to look in on Sue's computer screen. She's new and you need to keep an eye on her work. You see that she is working on a letter using a word processor. You monitor her for awhile without interfering with her work. She doesn't even know you're there![13]

The advertisement goes on to explain that by using the program you can make the rounds of the company, hot keying from computer to computer, "Viewing one screen after another, helping some, watching others. All from the comfort of your chair. . . . Amazed, you think that support has never been this easy before."[14]

Any network administrator has largely the same capability as part of their "support" and maintenance functions. The point is that accessing a computer user's screen on a network can be relatively easy to do. Collecting information on private computers has become widespread using HTTP Cookies (packets of information sent by a server to a World Wide Web browser and then sent back by the browser each time it accesses that server), which beside providing user authentication can also provide information profiles on individuals and their computer use. Closely related is spyware which is designed to take control of a computer's operation without the permission of the computer's owner.

In the case of network surveillance, the term "support" is used as a euphemism for surveillance and control. C. A. Bowers describes how similar systems:

> used by an airline company collects data on how long each of its 400 reservation clerks spend on each call and how much time elapses before they pick up their next one. Workers earn negative points if they repeatedly use more than 109 seconds in handling a call or take more than 12 minutes in bathroom trips. Truck drivers have their performance monitored by a small computer aptly named Tripmaster. Speed, gear shifts, amount of time the engine idles, and time used for coffee breaks are all recorded on a printout. Even the key strokes of the typist can be electronically recorded, so that compensation can be exactly calibrated to performance. In one data-processing firm, for example, an employee who performs five keystrokes a second (18,000 per hour) earns the top salary.[15]

In her book *In the Age of the Smart Machine: The Future of Work and Power*, Shoshana Zuboff describes the effects of the use of "smart machines" (i.e., computers) to control the work done in various types of companies.[16] Zuboff argues that "computer-mediated work" is not neutral, but embodies "essential characteristics that are bound to alter the nature of work within our factories and offices, and among workers, professional and managers."[17] New technologies based on computers make it possible for management to invent "novel ways to enhance certainty and control while employees discover new methods of self-protection and even sabotage.[18]

Zuboff presents a series of case studies of how computers have the potential to fundamentally change the intrinsic character of work across a wide range of settings. She clearly recognizes that the assumptions underlying machine function and human function are essentially different. According to her: "Because machines are mute, and because they are precise and repetitive, they can be controlled according to a set of rational principles in a way that human bodies cannot."[19]

Observation in the work place—or the potential for observation—seriously alters how people approach their work. Zuboff describes a manager in a factory who uses a computer "Overview System" or monitoring system as a substitute for more personal contact with workers:

> If I didn't have the Overview System, I would walk around and talk to people more. I would make phone calls and digress, like asking someone about their family. I would be more interested in what people were thinking about and what stresses they were under. When I managed in another plant without it, I had a better feeling of the human dynamics.

Now we have all the data, but we don't know *why*. The system can't give you the heartbeat of the plant; it puts you out of touch.[20]

While the computerized "panoptic" system provides one type of information on a comprehensive basis, it excludes other information sources that may be equally important in the effective management of a plant.

The Integrity of Data in a Post-Typographic Culture

Winston Smith, the main character in George Orwell's *1984*, had a job in the Ministry of Truth—to rewrite the past. Historical information was altered to suit changing political trends and needs. Offending passages and names were eliminated from existing texts. Books and newspapers were recalled and rewritten.

In a pre-computer culture, rewriting history book by book was not realistic. Rewriting a book, so that "undesirable" information is edited out, was extremely time-consuming and not always thorough enough. In a digital culture, the alteration of text becomes much simpler. Anyone who has used a word-processor with a search and delete function knows how easy it is to alter data. A name can be searched throughout an entire record and modified or eliminated with the touch of a few keystrokes.

As we enter more and more of our information onto massive databases, it will become easier to control and manipulate the historical record, as well as what type of information people have access to. Recently in China, search engines such as Google under the direction of the government limited access to sites the government deemed undesirable for its citizens. These include Falun Gong (a Buddhist group) and pro-democracy websites.[21]

That a repressive political regime such as that found in Communist China would take advantage of the ability to control information to its own advantage is not surprising. This book, for example, could be searched for undesirable comments such as the one found in the previous sentence. Such comments could very easily be eliminated from online information systems easily. All of the writing by a politically suspect author could automatically be purged from a system. Or, selected works might only be available to selected individuals. The alteration of digitally coded information is not limited to just textual sources. Photographs now can be altered using computers. A whole new area of "image processing" has developed in the field of architecture, in which a photograph is digitally altered in order to show how a particular design will affect a specific setting. Using such technologies, a planning board or city commission can "see" what a proposed project will look like when it is completed.

What must be remembered, however, is that a digitally constructed photograph is a simulation. As such it has a specific point of view and perspective, one that may emphasize certain selected characteristics. In this context some of Ted Nelson's ideas in *Computer Lib* are extremely helpful. According to Nelson:

Every simulation program, and thus every simulation, has a *point of view*. Just like a statement in words about the world, it is a *model* of how things are with its own implicit emphases: it highlights some things, omits others, and always simplifies.[22]

Digital photography also has the potential to seriously distort reality. In a review of Fred Richtin's book *In Our Own Image: The Coming Revolution in Photography*,[23] *Newsweek* magazine asked graphic artist Robert Bowen to construct a digitally altered photograph of different celebrities and world leaders, including Ronald Reagan, Queen Elizabeth II, Elvis Presley, Moimar Kadafi and Marla Maples. Using Pixar and Sun Systems together with an Apple Macintosh, Bowen created, from five separate portraits, a convincing composite photograph of the group at an imaginary dinner banquet.[24]

Actually, photographic sources have always been subject to alteration and manipulation. Such alterations, however, were difficult to do and relatively easy to detect. In a digital context, the alteration of photographic information is relatively easy to accomplish and almost impossible to detect. Fred Richtin refers to this whole area of digital photography as "hyper-photography."[25] This equation of digital photography and the hypermedia phenomenon is well-taken. In an archival context, Richtin argues that:

> The current move to make reference libraries of photographs more accessible to computer searches (including the extensive holdings of the Library of Congress) will allow ever greater numbers of nineteenth- and twentieth-century images (including lantern slides and glass-plate negatives) to be made immediately available.[26]

Important issues of copyright arise in the context of hyper-photography. What are the rights of the original photographer who took an image? Does an editor have the right to do cosmetic or aesthetic alterations on a photograph? What rights does a photographer have to a composite picture in which his work is included? What happens to the integrity of photographs as historical documents? With hyper-photography, according to Richtin, photography will become "more variegated, less an automatic validation of the way things are."[27]

Traditional art forms have the potential to become radically transformed, presenting some remarkable possibilities for the near future. In the 2002 movie *Simone*, a movie director Viktor Taransky, played by Al Pacino, replaces a temperamental actress who has dropped out of one of his films with a computer generated character named Simone (literally "Simulation One"), who is a composite of the great movie actresses of all time. Taransky's simulation immediately becomes an international sensation. While creating computer generated actors may seem like science fiction, it is almost certainly a possibility for the future.

Computer Control in Contemporary Society

Two social control issues emerge from the introduction of networked computer technology in our own culture. The first involves the potential to create a panoptic society based on the principles of observation and control. The second concerns the distortion and alteration of data for the purposes of establishing or maintaining social control. These are not simply academic issues, but are at the very heart of a moral and ethical debate concerning the role of computers in the definition of an emerging post-typographic culture. In this context, Terry Winograd and Fernando Flores argue that:

> The concern about what computers can do is not an abstract conundrum to be puzzled over for intellectual amusement, but a practical question at the center of a significant discourse in society as a whole. The answer as understood by the public (including those who make political and business decisions) is ultimately more significant than the twists and turns of academic debate. Dealing with the understanding that appears in the public discourse about computing, we can better achieve what we have set out to do—to reveal the pre-understanding we and others bring to computer technology and by doing so to open a new clearing in which to glimpse future paths for design.[28]

Computer systems, depending on how they are designed and used, have the potential to seriously limit our personal freedoms and the rights guaranteed us under the First Amendment. We need to fully take into account how the nature of networked computer systems contribute to the potential for the panoptic principles of surveillance and control to be enacted. Computers, as J. David Bolter has pointed out, represent a controlling technology. As he explains:

> Computers perform no work themselves; they direct work. The technology of "command and control," as Norbert Wiener has aptly named it, is of little value without something to control, generally other machines whose function is to perform work. For example, the essence of the American space shuttle is the computers that control almost every phase of its operation. But unless the powerful rocket engines provide the expected thrust, there is no mission for the computers to control. The computer leaves intact many older technologies particularly the technologies of

power, and yet inputs them in a new perspective. With the appearance of a truly subtle machine like the computer, the old power machines (steam, gas, or rocket engines) lose something of their prestige. Power machines are no longer agents on their own, subject only to direct human intervention; now they must submit to the hegemony of the computer that coordinates their effects.[29]

We are faced with the very real danger of having our intellectual and personal freedoms subjected to the "hegemony of the computer." If we, for example, design hypermedia curriculums for students that create an "audit trail" of their keystrokes and inquiries, then we must be sure that this record is not used for the purposes of surveillance and control. Who accesses a computer network, and what type of information is pursued, is just as much a freedom in a democratic society as the right to free speech and access to a broad range of knowledge without interference or censorship. The threat posed by hypertext and hypermedia technologies is that they provide the potential technology for significant surveillance and control. It is a well-known axiom that available technologies tend to be employed. In the case of hypertext and hypermedia systems, surveillance and control functions that limit personal freedoms and liberties must be avoided at all costs as they combine to work together with the other elements found in the Difference Engine.

Notes

1. George Orwell, *1984* (New York: Signet Library, 1961).

2. *Ibid.*, pp. 6-7.

3. The idea of the computer as providing the basis around which an electronic panopticon can develop was an original idea to me when I wrote the first draft of this essay. Its power as an idea is indicated by the fact that the image is one that has been picked up independently by other authors as well. See, for example, Chapter 9, "The Information Panopticon," pp. 315-361 and Chapter 10, "Panoptic Power and the Social Text," pp. 362-386, in Shoshana Zuboff's *In the Age of the Smart Machine: The Future of Work and Power* (New York: Basic Books, 1988) and C. A. Bowers in his section entitled "Computers and the Panopticon Society," pp. 14-19 in his work *The Cultural Dimensions of Educational Computing: Understanding the Non-Neutrality of Technology* (New York: Teachers College Press, 1988).

4. My use of the term *frame* is based upon the work of the British sociologist Erving Goffman and more specifically his work *Frame Analysis: An Essay on the Organization of Human Experience* (New York: Harper and Row, 1974). Bowers, in *The Cultural Dimensions of Educational Computing*, pp. 24-27 draws on Goffman and frame analysis as part of his analysis of the cultural dimension of educational computing. Among Bowers's most compelling arguments is that the supporters of educational computing by: "providing the metaphorical language considered appropriate for thinking about the educational uses of the microcomputer, . . . controlled the frame that governed the discourse and thus the context for thinking about the educational potential of this new technology." (*Ibid.*, p. 25)
   Marshall McLuhan makes a similar point when he argues in *Understanding Media* that: "Technological environments are not merely passive containers of people but are active processes that reshape people and other technologies alike." See: McLuhan, *Understanding Media: The Extensions of Man* (New York: Mentor Books, 1964), p. 1v.

5. Michel Foucault, *Discipline and Punish*, translated by Alan Sheridan (New York: Random House, 1979), p. 2.

6. Jeremy Bentham, *Panopticon; or, the Inspection-House: Containing the Idea of a New Principle of Construction Applicable to Any Sort of Establishment, In Which Persons of Any Description Are to be Kept Under Inspection: And in Particular to Penitentiary-Houses, Prisons, Poor Houses, Lazarettos, Houses of Industry, Manufactories, Hospitals, Work-Houses, Mad-Houses, and Schools: With a Plan of Management Adapted to the Principles: In a Series of Letters, Written in the Year 1787, from Crecheff in White Russia, To a Friend in England, Included in The Works of Jeremy Bentham*, Volume Four, ed. John Bowring (New York: Russell & Russell, Inc., 1962), title page.

7. *Ibid.*, p. 40.

8. Foucault, *Discipline and Punishment*, p. 200.

9. *Ibid.*

10. Bowers, *The Cultural Dimensions of Educational Computing*, p. 15.

11. *Ibid.*

12. *Ibid.*, p. 16.
13. Advertisement in *PC Week*, September 1989.
14. *Ibid.*
15. Bowers, *The Cultural Dimensions of Educational Computing*, p. 17.
16. Zuboff, *In the Age of the Smart Machine*.
17. *Ibid.*, p. 7.
18. *Ibid.*, p. 7.
19. *Ibid.*, p. 8.
20. *Ibid.*, p. 326.
21. Chris Oliver and John Shinal, "Google Will Censor New China Service." *MarketWatch*, January 25, 2006. Available archived online at: http://www.marketwatch.com/news/.
22. Ted Nelson, *Computer Lib* (Redmond, WA: Microsoft Press, 1987), p. 149.
23. Fred Richtin, *In Our Own Image: The Coming Revolution in Photography* (New York: Aperture, 1990).
24. Jonathan Alter, "When Photographs Lie," *Newsweek*, July 30, 1990, pp. 44 and 46.
25. Richtin, *In Our Own Image*, p. 141.
26. *Ibid.*, p. 68.
27. *Ibid.*, p. 100.
28. Terry Winograd and Fernando Flores, *Understanding Computers and Cognition*, (Massachusetts: Addison Wesley Publishing Compnay, 1987), p. xiii.
29. J. David Bolter, *Turning's Man: Western Culture in the Computer Age*, (Chapel Hill: The University of North Carolina Press, 1984), p. 8.

Chapter 7

Mobile Computing

Illustration of a dynabook as proposed by Alan Kaye in 1972. Courtesy of Theresa Bramblett.

Mobile computing represents the newest element of the Difference Engine. For the purposes of this book, mobile computing refers to the use of cell phones, digital assistants, notebook computers, tablet computers and wearable computers. In the near future, mobile computers will almost certainly include devices that at the present time are only described in science fiction, or in the theoretical works of computer and robotic scientists.

It is likely that these future devices will include neural jacks that will allow the user to plug their consciousness into a computer data set and download information, commonplace event in novels such as William Gibson's *Neuromancer*[1] and *Mona Lisa Overdrive*.[2] As incredible as such a scenario seems, human machine interfaces are already underway with experimentation involving everything from artificial retinas to restore the sight of blind people to cochlear implants to restore lost hearing. In Vernor Vinge's, *Rainbow's End*, wearable computer (literally built into clothes) are used by a wide-range of people, as are contact lenses that project information onto the retina.[3]

In fact, wearable computers in the form of medical devices have been in use since the 1960s. In their most basic forms, they include technologies such as insulin pumps and heart monitors. Computers are now being developed using nanotube carbon technology that involves the layering of flexible batteries into clothing. Processors and display systems can be woven into the cloth making it possible to have wearable computersy. What their potential uses are is still unknown—possibly dynamic lit emitting cloth that could change color or present a written message or photograph. Perhaps a coded system that would alert the wearer of a group membership (imagine a combat group wearing coordinated body armor) and so on.[4]

Cell Phones and Mobile Computing

The United Nations estimates that by mid 2010 there will be five billion cell phone subscribers in the world, out of a total population of 6 billion people. These numbers are extraordinary, suggesting a revolution in instant communication and connectivity of the type anticipated by McLuhan with his "global village." It is a revolution of what is essentially universal computing. The reality that is emerging is every cell phone is not only a telephonic device, but also potentially a computer.

In 2010, mobile broadband subscribers will number one billion people worldwide. Computing in the form of cell phones makes access to the Internet and World Wide Web possible for those in the most remote places, as well as those with limited resources. Cell phones are inexpensive. They can be easily recharged with solar power. In Africa, for example, there are numerous kiosks where phones can be rented or subscriptions purchased.[5]

Cell phones have become constant companions for people. They are with their owners almost wherever they go. They make connectivity and information available on a constant basis. Currently, cell phone interface devices are limited to the phone and earphone, voice-activated and mike devices. It seems inevitable that increasingly subtle interfaces will develop that allow commands to be carried out through retinal movement, hand movements and even sub-vocal sounds.

Nowhere is the confusion over whether a cell phone is a telephonic device or a computer clearer than in case of Apple Corporation's iPhone, which incorporates elements of full-blown desktop and portable computer systems into machines within screens one tenth the size of a laptop computer screen. iPhone's connect easily into mobile broadband networks. They include an almost limitless number of tools and technical devices from stopwatches to international time zone clocks, from global satellite positioning systems to texting systems, electronic books, media players and games.

Personal habits can be tracked via a cell phone ranging from eating habits, to blood glucose levels and blood pressure. Using a program such as *your.flowingdata* (http://yourflowingdata.com) via Twitter (the social networking and microblogging system) data is entered from almost any location. Once delivered to *your. flowingdata*, it can be compiled and put into graphs that show an individual's behavior over time (eating habits, sleep patterns, exercise routines, etc.).[6]

Cell phones as computers, however, are inherently limited simply by their size, a problem which is rapidly being addressed by the development of easily portable, and highly functional, tablet computers. Of these systems, none seems to have as more promise than the recently released Apple iPad.

Tablet Computing as a New Component of the Difference Engine

Tablet computing was first discussed by the computer pioneer, Alan Kaye, in 1968. Kaye was interested in making "A Personal Computer for Children of All Ages."[7] Called a Dynabook, Kay's device was intended primarily for use by children. It combined elements of both laptop and tablet computers. Fundamental to the idea of the device was portability and ease of use.

Kaye described the device as follows:

> The size should be no larger than a notebook, weight less than 4lbs; the visual display should be able to present at least 4000 *printing quality* characters with contrast ratios approaching that of a book, dynamic graphics of reasonable quality should be possible; there should be removable local file storage of at least one million characters (about 500 ordinary pages) traded off against several hours of audio (voice/music) file. . . . A combination of this "carry anywhere" device and a global information ultility such as the ARPA network of two-way cable TV, will bring the libraries and schools (not to mention stores and billboards) of the world to the home. One can imagine one of the first programs an owner will write is a filter to eliminate advertising.[8]

The iPhone has the essential functions (and many more) of Kaye's dynabook. Its processing speed, story capacity, connectivity and portability, however, is far beyond anything that Kaye was describing. The iPhone has a full keyboard capability for texting and a highly effective touch screen that allows it to be manipulated by simply touching it with one's fingers. The main problem with the iPhone, however, has been its screen size. Measuring only 2 by 3 inches, the iPhone does not lend itself to reading long selections of text, nor to viewing photographic material or movies. Apple Corporation addressed the problem by building virtually all of the functions of an iPhone into its iPad system. It has a screen that measures approximately 6 by 9 inches, or approximately ten times the size of an iPhone.

Illustration of the home screen for an iPad . Courtesy of Glenn Fleishman and Wikipedia Creative Commons.

The results are remarkable. The device is one that bears a remarkable resemblance to Kaye's dynabook. It is possible, for example, to have a keyboard appear on the screen that is roughly the same size as the keyboard of a notebook computer. Videos can be viewed easily, as can text for electronic books. The device, like the iPhone, can be used in portrait or landscape mode—the latter providing a broader image. As an electronic book, the iPad makes it possible to provide high-end color graphics in the form of photographs, animations and movies into traditional text. In addition, it is possible to connect whatever appears on the device's screen to the Internet, and portability. For the first time a portable electronic book reader with full Internet connectivity, color, high level audio and multimedia functions, as well as an extended battery time of approximately ten hours.

How important is this? Assuming that the iPad is the first highly interactive, color multimedia electronic book, it revolutionizes book functions. Book content can be delivered via mobile band networks or local wi-fi systems. While systems such as Amazon's Kindle delivers books via cell phone broadcast, it does so to a much more limited black and white machine. With the Apple iPad, it becomes possible to include video, animation and sound embedded into the text. As a result, key terms in a textbook can be highlighted, and defined with spoken definitions. Animations to explain a complex physical principal in physics, or a dance movement can be included, as can classic film clips in a history of cinematography textbook, or a walk through an historical site or museum in a history book. Students can connect to other students. It is conceivable to have mass study and review groups for students using the same electronic textbook across various universities and colleges.

While all of the above functions have existed in the form of laptop and net book computers, in the tablet computer, the technology that has been available for some years actually functions. Parallels with the Gutenberg revolution of the fifteenth century come to mind. Essentially, the technology of the book—i.e. ,printed pages on paper bound together—dates back to the late twelfth century. Paper was available in Europe for several hundred years prior to Gutenberg. What made the difference with Gutenberg's invention was that he combined multiple technologies together to create a new technology (printing press, paper manufacture, type casting and design). The result was a technological and cultural revolution. While the iPad is certainly not a revolution comparable to Gutenberg's innovation, it may be the medium that provides the essential technology configuration that makes the mobile electronic multimedia book possible. In doing so, it transforms publishing, and quite likely the very ways we teach and learn

Mobile Computing and Social Networking

Social networking has emerged as ubiquitous technology during the last decade. Internet based programs such as MySpace, Facebook and Friendster, connect people together who have shared interests and activities. Mobile computing clearly intensifies these systems. This is particularly evident with programs such as Twitter, which allows the user to send brief messages, no longer than 140 characters, to subscribers anywhere, anytime. An author or pundit can broadcast his or her thoughts on a virtually continuous basis, from any location at any time. A movie star can keep his or her fans posted on their every thought and activity.

We are not far enough into the mobile computing revolution to understand the implications of all of this. Twitter, for example, may end up being nothing more than a fad, allowing people to keep themselves and their ideas constantly in front of a selected audience. It may, however, have profound uses in education and training, as well as alter the nature of how cliques and social groups operate in settings such as high schools.

For selected groups, the importance of texting, whether in the form of Twitter or I-Message, cannot be overemphasized. Suddenly the telephone (a device almost totally excluded from use by the profoundly deaf) becomes an extraordinarily powerful tool for those interested in communicating with the hearing or non-hearing population.

*   *   *

The implications of mobile computing for society and education are only just beginning to be understood. What is clear is that we are experiencing the creation of yet another component of the Difference Engine. Like each of other components described in this book (*Hypertext/Hypermedia*; *Augmented Intelligence*; *Networked Information and Communication Systems*; *Collective Intelligence*; *Hyperreality*; and the *Panoptic Sort*), mobile computing is yet another component of the evolving machinery that creates the Engine.

Notes

1. William Gibson, *Neuromancer* (New York: Ace Science Fiction, 1984).

2. William Gibson, *Mona Lisa Overdrive* (New York: Victor Gollancz Limited, 1988).

3. Vernor Vinge, *Rainbow's End: A Novel with One Foot in the Future* (New York: Tor Books, 2006).

4. BBC World News American, "Carbon Nanotubes Used to Make Batteries from Fabric." Available online from: http://www.in.com/news/science-technology/fullstory-carbon-nanotubes-used-to-make-batteries-from-fabrics-12502877-in-1.html (Accessed February 14, 2010)

5. Editorial, "The Revolution Has Gone Mobile," *The New York Times*, February 19, 2010.

6. Steve Lohr, "Smart Dust? Not Quite, but We're Getting There," *The New York Times*, January 30, 2010 online edition.

7. David Kaye, "A Personal Computer for Children of All Ages. In Proceedings of the ACM National Conference, Boston Aug. 1972." Accessed online at: http://mprove.de/diplom/gui/kay72.html.

8. *Ibid.*

Chapter 8

Reinventing the Text

Illustration from *The Book of Job* (1825) by the English engraver and poet William Blake.

Historically, new technologies have provided the potential to create new forms of art. As they emerge, it is virtually impossible to predict the artistic possibilities inherent in them. Who could have imagined that the invention of glass would lead to the creation of an artistic vision such as the Rose Window at Chartres? Did the artists/chemists who invented oil paints have any notion that their experiments would result in works such as Rembrandt's "The Night Watch"?

In our own era, new literary and visual art forms are being made possible through the innovative use of computers. New technologies are creating new forms of art and literature. Traditionally independent mediums such as print, sound recording, motion pictures, video and animation are being merged in multimedia computer and Internet based systems. Innovations such as tablet computers can now deliver these elements in products such as electronic books easily and at minimal cost.

On the Internet and the World Wide Web a new type of electronic writing is coming into being as authors connect text and pictorial information with other sites spread around the world. In addition, writing now has the potential to become a collective process—readers becoming authors as they add to a text created by a single author.

In the following chapter, I explore how visual and animated language is creating new forms of literature and art. Artistic creations of this type are important because they are frequently the testing ground for new technologies and cultural models. Everything that I will be describing is possible with existing, and relatively inexpensive, computer systems. Most of the technologies necessary— including virtual reality—are available "off the shelf."

Animating Text

Visual and animated languages are obviously not new concepts. The ancient Egyptians, with their use of hieroglyphics, were among the first people to use this artistic form. In Chinese dialects such as Mandarin, calligraphic forms take on motion and meaning through the sweep of brush strokes on rice paper. The symbol for man resembles the shape of a human being. During the Middle Ages, elaborate illuminated texts extended the pictorial element of letters and words. Text and image merged during the late eighteenth century in the works of the poet William Blake and in the middle of the nineteenth century with the writings of Lewis Carroll.

More recently visual language has been explored by poets such as Stéphane Malarmé, whose 1897 book of poems presented a new type of "visual poetry" where words and letters were arranged in a non-linear manner to create different patterns and designs. At the same time that Malarmé was experimenting with his visual poems, Jean Arp and Tristan Tzara experimented with poems that were not only visually "concrete," but often employed random elements for their

so that her idea of the tale was something like
this :———"Fury said to
          a mouse, That
                    he met
                        in the
                            house,
                        ' Let us
                        both go
                        to law :
                  I will
            prosecute
          you.—
          Come, I 'll
              take no
                  denial ;
                      We must
                          have a
                                  trial :
                                      For
                                  really
                                  this
                                  morning
                                          I 've
                                  nothing
                              to do.'
                      Said the
                      mouse to
                      the cur,
                        ' Such a
                              trial,
                          dear sir,
                      With no
                  jury or
                  judge.
                  would be
                      wasting
                          our breath.
                              ' I 'll be
                          judge.
                      I 'll be
                  jury,'
                  said
                      cunning
                          old Fury,
                              ' I 'll try
                                  the whole
                                      cause,
                                          and
                                      condemn
                                  you
                              to
                                  death.

construction.[1]

Obviously the computer can be used to generate words, either randomly or according to some pre-established algorithm (based on rhyme, meter and so on). The Nobel laureate Octavio Paz has argued in his essay "The New Analogy: Poetry and Technology" that: "There is no reason why the poet shouldn't use a computer to choose and combine the words that are to make up his poem."[2] For Paz the computer is a tool, much as the saw and hammer are tools for the cabinetmaker, which can help the poet discover new aspects of language and the relationship between words:

> The computer no more does away with the poet than do dictionaries of rhyme or treatises on rhetoric. The computer poem is the result of a mechanical process somewhat comparable to the mental and verbal operations that a seventeenth-century courtier in the West had to go through in order to write a sonnet, or those that a Japanese of the same century performed in order to compose, with a group of friends, the collective poems called *haikai no renga*.[3]

According to Paz, poetry thus becomes "a creative deviation that produces a new and different order."[4]

> Poetry enters the picture at the moment when impersonal memory—the vocabulary of the computer or the dictionary—and our personal memory intersect: suspension of the rules and irruption of the unexpected and unpredictable. A break in the usual procedure, an end to formula—poetry is *always* an alteration, a linguistic deviation.[5]

A simple example of a new order of poetry based on using the computer can be accomplished by using combinatorial principles to create a new type of branching poetry. This can be explained by using the analogy of a popular parlor toy from the nineteenth century—"dissected" or "sliced" portraits. This toy consisted of portraits divided into three sections (upper [eyes], middle [nose] and lower [mouth]). Three original portraits could be rearranged to create twenty-seven different portraits. The combinations and permutations increase exponentially as more new portraits are added. The end result is that a relatively small number of illustrations can produce literally millions of combinatorial possibilities.

This principle can be applied to the writing of poetry in a hypertext or hypermedia context. Take, for example, the following traditional three-part haiku poem in which the first and last lines are five syllables and the second line is seven syllables.

1   I felt her eyes look
1A   at me as if I were a
1B   love long forgotten.

This poem could be combined with the following poem.

2   She could not help look
2A   my way as though I were a
2B   moment of love lost.

The resulting combination would create four new poems.

1   I felt her eyes look
1A   at me as if I were a
2B   moment of love lost.

1   I felt her eyes look
2A   my way as though I were a
2B   moment of love lost.

2   She could not help look
2A   my way as though I were a
1B   love long forgotten.

2   She could not help look
1A   at me as if were a
1B   love long forgotten.

Two carefully crafted and psychologically interrelated hypermedia poems would have the potential to create four new expressions out of the two original poems. Three poems combined together could create twelve poems, and so on.

Assuming that a gifted poet could create three interrelated poems about a single topic, the combinations and permutations could then be combined together to literally create a book-length work. In a sufficiently well-crafted series of poems, all of the combinatorial poems would have the potential for significant meaning and psychological complexity. The creation of a combinatorial poem of this type could represent a new literary form.

Suppose, for a moment, that the model outlined above also includes not simply combinatorial factors but a typeface or dynamic font that changes according to specific algorithms. Thus, in the sentence "The words went up and down the page," they would actually do so:

The words went up and down the page,

In the sentence "It isn't over until the fat lady sings," it would be possible to have the letters in the word *lady* actually become fat. In the sentence "The brown dog jumped over the fence," the words *brown dog* could actually jump over the word *fence*. This could happen automatically or it could be activated by a linking hypermedia button.

In the case of a combinatorial poem of the type described earlier, new configurations could also alter the dynamic font. Look at the following haikus.

1   The dog on the step
1A   his black coat like coal on fire
1B   shining as he sleeps.

2   The cat lies at my feet
2A   his white fur like fresh crisp snow
2B   waiting to be stroked.

Four new poems are created through the combinatorial process. Using the dynamic font each one creates different visualizations. In poem 1/1A/2b the dog's fur is black. In poem 1/2A/2B the dog's fur is white.

1   The dog on the step
1A   his black coat like coal on fire
2B   waiting to be stroked.

1   The dog on the step
2A   his white fur like fresh crisp snow
2B   waiting to be stroked.
2   The cat lies at my feet
2A   his white fur like fresh crisp snow
1B   shining as he sleeps.
2   The cat lies at my feet
2A   his black coat like coal on fire
1B   shining as he sleeps.

In an electronic medium, with a virtually unlimited spectrum of colors and animation formats available, it becomes an easy task to present the poem in its different formats. The colored and animated quality of the dynamic text becomes lost, however, when printed. This suggests that such forms will ultimately have to be presented either on computer screens or in dynabooks—small but extremely powerful computers—that have the convenience of size and portability of a book, but have full computational powers.

Using the computer in this way creates a new poetic space—one that can have temporal and cinematic qualities. This is an essential element of poetry according to Paz, who argues that the substance from which poetry "is made of is time."[6] The printed page, like the Chinese scroll, represents "metaphors of time," of "space in motion." For Paz a poem literally means speaking and hearing with one's eyes:

> on the day that someone finally decides to make full use of cinematographic resources, it will also be possible to combine reading and hearing, written signs and sounds. The screen is a multiple page that engenders other pages: a wall, column, or stele, it is a single immense canvas across which a text might be inscribed in a movement analogous to, though the reverse of, that of a Chinese scroll unfolding.[7]

Paz believes that the computer can take poetry "back to its origin, to what it was in the beginning: the spoken word, shared by a group."[8]

The use of the computer to create new formats for poetry radically changes the traditional authority of the poetic form. As William Dickey argues:

> At this point we confront an aesthetic question that has been much in evidence in twentieth-century poetry: whether the reality of the poem lies in its fixed printed form, a continuous and unchanging authority, or whether the poem becomes real each time it is performed, recited from memory, on a stage by its author, or experienced in the simulated performance in which we hear the spoken language behind the text we are scanning on the printed page. As soon as we move away from textual and graphic elements in the poem, as soon as we introduce such elements as randomization, or sound, or animation, we have arrived at a work of art for which the page is no longer an adequate representation; at best the page can provide a kind of vocal or orchestral score for the poem, and even there its nature will be limiting and misleading, as it enforces its own qualities of linearity and singleness on works that are no longer governed by those qualities.[9]

For Dickey, computers using hypertext and hypermedia have the potential to transform poetry and fiction by opening:

> new possibilities of interplay between modes of representation, as it departs from linearity and the authority of text into association and performance, it may generate conceptions of form which have elements in common with those

upon which oral transmission of literature has been dependent: the riddle, the circular epic journey.[10]

There is a certain irony in the fact that as we proceed farther into a post-typographic culture, we may be introducing literary forms that are closer to pre-typographic rather than typographic forms of literacy.

It may be that a glimpse of what Paz proposed can be seen in Peter Greenway's interpretation of Shakespeare's *The Tempest*. In his 1991 film *Prospero's Books* Greenway used new computer-based technologies to combine animation, film and music. In doing so, he managed to blur the line between literature and film. Converting traditional 35 millimeter film to high definition video, Greenaway manipulated his images in *Prospero's Books* with the aid of a computer and then converted the results back into film, which gave him the ability to communicate information at a much higher density than is available using more traditional cinematic, or as was the case with Shakespeare in the original *Tempest*, typographic forms. The process was described by the late film critic Bill Cosford as one in which Greenaway "illuminates and expands the screen. . . . He pumps his images with the whole array, all working at the same time. He lays moving images within others and more within them. He writes on the frame, animates the subjects of the books and converts the live action subjects back into a kind of literature."[11]

The Quantel Paint System that Greenway used to manipulate and create many of the images for the film is a hypermedia system—a subset of hypertext. While the viewer's screen is not interactive, it is clear that Greenaway's cinematic vision is dependent on connected frames and overlays and is strongly influenced by hypertext and hypermedia principles.

Greenway's work in *Prospero's Books* moves film toward text, while hypermedia authoring programs such as Macromedia's *Director* and Adobe's Flash use the metaphor of a film script to create hypermedia programs that incorporate both cinematic and text elements. Director blurs the line between film and text and can be used with relatively little difficulty to create new symbolic/iconic writing systems for the composition of poetry. The types of word experiments undertaken by Mallarmé could now undergo another evolution.

Imagine putting on "computer clothing," which includes devices such as eye-phones (a tiny pair of video screens that are mounted in front of each eye that provide stereo vision of a computer-created reality), data gloves (in which sensors lining your hand communicate movement to a graphics computer) and stereo earphones and positional sensing equipment, with which you can enter a simulated computer environment.[12]

Using such a system, a poem could be made that surrounded the individual in a sensorium of sound and animated effects. Similar techniques and principles could be incorporated to create new types of interactive novels that draw heavily on video game and simulation techniques in addition to traditional print forms.

The creation of new artistic forms as discussed above, while on one level extremely promising, also poses a number of disturbing possibilities. It is easy to imagine the creation of new artistic forms similar to Huxley's "feelies" in his novel *Brave New World*.

Whatever the case, it is clear that a new artistic medium is emerging—one that has the potential to merge text, sound, video, film and objects in ways we can only begin to imagine. This is particularly the case in terms of the creation of new forms of interactive literature—ones that are dependent upon the technologies provided by computers and networked systems—i.e., the Difference Engine.

Interactive Literature

Examples of interactive literature can be found in a number of fictional sources. In a wonderful short story published in the mid-1970s for *The New Yorker* magazine entitled "The Kuglemass Episode," Woody Allen describes how a shy and introverted middle-aged professor longs for romance. He is helped by a magician who has a magical box that allows the user to place himself in a book, on any page you chose. Kuglemass decides to enter into Flaubert's novel *Madame Bovary*, where he has an affair with the main character, Emma. Kuglemass stays in the novel until Emma meets Rodolphe and the competition for her affection begins to get a bit too rough, at which point Kuglemass returns to real life.[13]

The type of scenario outlined by Woody Allen in "The Kuglemass Episode" is in fact increasingly possible as a result of emerging technologies such as hypermedia and virtual reality. As Jay David Bolter and Michael Joyce have pointed out, interactive fiction has existed for some time in the form of computer adventure games.[14] Games such as *Zork*, which was introduced during the mid-1980s, allows the player to assume various roles and experience adventures including looking for hidden objects, fighting monsters or collecting treasure. More recent games such as *Myst*, and even much maligned "First-Person Shooter" games such as *Grand Theft Auto 2* incorporate similar principles as well. Bolter and Joyce argue that:

> Even the simplest of these games is a fictional hypertext. For the computer is presenting the player with a text, and the player's job is to understand and respond to that text. Depending upon his response, the computer presents more text and awaits a further response. The player, then, is an unusually powerful reader, whose decisions determine what text he will next see.[15]

It is significant that while the text in computer games is "simple-minded," its presentation is highly sophisticated and represents a type of hypertext or hypermedia.[16]

Hypertext has been defined as "the use of the computer to transcend the linear, bounded and fixed qualities of the traditional written text."[17] Likewise, interactive fiction as a type of hypertext transcends the bounded and fixed qualities of traditional text." A traditional story or novel is linear in nature. It proceeds from one point to another as determined by its author. Interactive fiction, in contrast, is non-linear. In its simplest form it includes two elements: 1. episodes, and 2. decision points between episodes.[18]

Decision points are the equivalent of links between episodes. In Stuart Moulthrop's computer novel *Chaos*, the reader sees the door to a house and hears eerie music and the noise from a party going on inside the house. As you enter the house, the computer screen turns into a page of text and you discover that you are at a party attended by mystics, robot designers, ghostwriters and other assorted people. Navigational arrows allow you to advance forward or backward through various text panels describing the party. Bordering the text on each panel are portraits of different people attending the event. You can click on and off these portraits with a mouse. Activating a portrait takes you into a separate story about that individual character.[19]

The development of interactive fiction is also leading to the creation of new hypermedia systems for composing stories. Jay David Bolter, John B. Smith and Michael Joyce, for example, some years ago developed a program called *Storyspace*, which was specifically designed for writing interactive fiction. *Storyspace* has an author's and a reader's mode. Using a structural editor, the author is able to create a series of textual episodes. The structural editor provides the author with a map or diagrammatic view of the hypertext he or she is creating. By activating a button or typing a command, the reader can direct the computer to follow different branches of the story. Storyspace has been described as turning "the straight line of old plots into a road map. At their most complex, these pieces become layers of maps and maps within maps."[20]

Ted Nelson identifies works such as Sterne's *Tristram Shandy*, Master's *Spoon River Anthology*, Cortazar's *Hopscotch*, Nabokov's *Pale Fire* and Proust's *Remembrance of Things Past* as being novels with hypertext principles at work in them.[21] In *Tristram Shandy*, for example, Sterne sees himself engaged in a conversation with his reader.

> As no one, who knows what he is about in good company, would venture to talk all;—so no author, who understands the just boundaries of decorum and good-breeding, would presume to think all: The truest respect which you can pay to a reader's understanding, is to halve this matter amicably, and leave him something to imagine, in his turn, as well as yourself.[22]

Sterne sees his reader shaping his work—literally contributing along with the author to its construction. In *Writing Space* Jay David Bolter argues that this participatory function in *Tristram Shandy* anticipates "electronic writing" in a number of important ways:

Sterne is a topographic writer, whose achievement is more remarkable because he works in the intractable medium of print. Insisting on a conversation with his reader, Sterne is contravening the natural use of print. In a playful way, he is inviting the reader to give up his or her safe status as reader and share responsibility for the narrative. Electronic writing puts the reader in the same position.[23]

For Bolter, the electronic writing space provided by new mediums such as hypertext and hypermedia provide a rich field for experimentation. Students of James Joyce, for example, could

> begin to map the network of references in a chapter of *Ulysses* or *Finnegan's Wake*. Each sentence or even each word might be made a topical unit in the electronic writing space. These units would first be connected in temporal order as they appear in print; further links could then be drawn to indicate allusions and parallels. The result would be a massive network that the scholar and even casual reader (can there be such a creature for *Ulysses* or *Finnegan's Wake?*) could traverse in a variety of ways. The reader could begin by reading the text in temporal order and then choose to follow a reference to some other part of the book.[24]

As new allusions are discovered by the reader, they are added to the system. Bolter makes clear that working through an electronic edition of Joyce would not be the same as reading a printed edition of his work. Instead, it would involve "the reading of readings—both watching and becoming the ideal reader of Joyce in the act of reading, a literary and a literary-critical experience at the same time."[25]

Of any modern author, perhaps none anticipates the possibilities of the electronic book and electronic writing as much as Jorge Luis Borges. In *Ficciones*, Borges writes a series of short pieces that are ideally suited for a hypertext or hypermedia format. In "An Examination of the Work of Herbert Quain," Borges provides a literary obituary for a writer who attempted to liberate his work from traditional linear forms. The thirteen chapters of Quain's work represent nine permutations of a series of events occurring over three evenings. In Borges's more complex work "The Garden of Forking Paths," the character Ts'ui Pen retires from public life with two purposes in mind: 1. to write a book, and 2. to build a labyrinth garden. Borges describes his work as "an enormous game, or parable, in which the subject is time." Borges's character Ts'ui Pen believed that time represented an ever-expanding "ever spreading network of diverging, converging and parallel times."[26]

Borges did not have access to a computer. But his ideas clearly fit a hypertext model. Stuart Moulthrop, the author of *Chaos*, has in fact taken Borges's "Garden of Forking Paths" and developed it as a Storyspace module of over one hundred units and three hundred connections or links. In addition, he has added his own material to the program.[27]

Interactive fiction can function in many different ways and on many different levels. Although the most obvious method to construct a hypertext story is to allow the reader choices that will set the plot in different directions, hypertext has the potential to present the same story from different points of view, or as part of a stream of consciousness technique.

In this context, an interactive story or novel operating in the freedom of an electronic environment would in many respects parallel the oral rather than written tradition of storytelling. The text of a story would have the potential to evolve as it moves through various readers and participants. If, as Walter Ong has argued, we lose much of the power of the oral world by accepting a textual world, hypertext and hypermedia have the potential to reintroduce that world to us—or at least one that has similar elements.[28]

Significantly, the pretextual or oral world was a world of magic. Fictional hypermedia universes—particularly ones augmented by virtual reality technology— have the potential to reintroduce magic into the world. Imagine an interactive novel in which a reader or participant can define his or her character. Such a scenario is in fact described by Vernor Vinge in his novella *True Names*. Vinge's system involves a "game" played on a national computer network. As he explains:

> The basic game was a distant relative of the ancient Adventure that had been played on computer systems for more than forty years, and a nearer relative of the participation novels that are still widely sold. There were two great differences though. This game was more serious, and was played at a level of complexity impossible without the use of the EEG input/output that the warlocks and the popular data bases called Portals.[29]

In *True Names*, the characters in the story—who are in fact highly sophisticated programmers—assume the powers of sorcerers and magicians within simulations they create for each other in the "Other Plane."

Interactive and hypermedia adventures do not need to function within the laws of the known physical world. Thus an individual in a simulation can be transformed into a dragon or a monster by invoking a special command or a set of spells (i.e., a programming sequence). Eventually, it will be possible to experience simulations that provide sophisticated sensory feedback. The "feelies" predicted by Aldous Huxley in *Brave New World* are clearly possible, and with them a simulated world subject to rules outlined within the gaming simulation defined by the computer.

In his novel *Fahrenheit 451*, Ray Bradbury imagined a possible scenario for participatory fiction. Mildred, the wife of the novel's main character, Guy Montag, explains how she is participating in a play that is projected as part of a sense-around or "wall-to-wall circuit" similar to some of the crude virtual reality simulators currently available:

this is a play (that) comes on the wall-to-wall circuit in ten minutes. They mailed me my part this morning. I sent in some boxtops. They write the script with one part missing. It's a new idea. The homemaker, that's me, is the missing part. When it comes time for the missing lines, they all look at me out of the three walls and I say the lines. . . . It's really fun. It'll be even more fun when we can afford to have the fourth wall installed.[30]

The potential for banal programming—not dissimilar to contemporary television soap operas—is obvious. Participatory feelies—predigested mini-versions of the classics are created for the masses. As Montag's supervisor Captain Beatty explains:

Classics cut to fit fifteen-minute radio shows, then cut again to fill a two-minute book column, winding up at last as a ten or twelve line dictionary resume. I exaggerate of course. The dictionaries were for reference. But many were those whose sole knowledge of *Hamlet* (you know the title certainly Montag; it is probably only a faint rumor of a title to you Mrs. Montag) whose sole knowledge, as I say, of *Hamlet* was a one page digest in a book that claimed: *now at last you can read all of the classics; keep up with your neighbors.* Do you see? Out of the nursery into the college and back into the nursery; there's your intellectual pattern for the past five centuries or more.[31]

Increasingly text, film and computer game become blurred. Peter Jackson's brilliant cinematic interpretation of J. R. R. Tolkien's *The Lord of the Rings* has generated several computer games, which not only incorporate the content of Tolkien's original text, but also of the films based on his writings. Classics in literature become transformed first into films, and then into interactive games.

What is much more likely to happen, rather than rewriting classics to fit the new hypermedia fictions, is that new works will be created. Such pieces have the potential to branch on a virtually infinite basis. Experimental films of this type were shown at the Czechoslovakian exhibit at Expo International—the World's Fair—that was held in Montreal in 1967. Essentially, viewers got to vote on different scenarios being advanced for the film they were viewing when certain nodal or turning points were reached. In a hypertext context, this corresponds to the user electing to link the segment of film they had watched to one of several possible plot lines.

Hypermedia fiction represents the potential fusion of text forms with media at almost every imaginable level and in almost every possible combination. The evolution of these forms to levels where they are considered great art may take many generations. It is worth noting that the novel did not immediately spring up as a literary form after the invention of moveable type. Despite the work of early figures such as Cervantes, it was not until the eighteenth century, and some would argue well into the nineteenth century, that the novel emerged as a major literary form. It seems reasonable to assume that the evolution of interactive and hypermedia fiction will also take place gradually rather than appear as a fully realized form.

What is clear is that a new literary form is emerging that fuses traditional text, film and video into an interactive and non-linear form that has the potential to be not just innovative, but revolutionary in nature—another example of the Analytical Engine at work.

Notes

1. Tzara, for example, gives the formula for this type of poem in one of his own works:

    To make a Dadaist poem.

    Take a newspaper.

    Take a pair of scissors.

    Choose an article as long as you are planning to make your poem.

    Cut out an article.

    Then cut out each of the words that make up the article and put them in a bag.

    Shake it gently.

    Then take out the scraps one after the other in the order in which they left the bag.

    Copy conscientiously.

    The poem will be like you.

    And here you are a writer, infinitely original, endowed with a sensibility that is charming, though beyond the understanding of the vulgar.

    In this context, the computer is ideally suited to randomly rearrange—or rearange in terms of all the possible combinations and permutations—a basic dictionary of words or even an existing poem.

    For discussions of Dadaist poetry see O. B. Hardison Jr. "Concrete Poetry," pp. 180-193 in *Disappearing Through the Skylight: Culture and Technology in the Twentieth Century* (New York: Penguin Books, 1989); and Jay David Bolter, *Writing Space: The Computer, Hypertext and the History of Writing* (Hillsdale, NJ: Lawrence Erlbaum, 1991), pp. 131 and 145.

2. Octavio Paz, "The New Analogy: Poetry and Technology," in *Convergences: Essays on Art and Literature*, translated from the Spanish by Helen Lane (San Diego: Harcourt Brace Jovanovich, 1987), pp. 124-125.

3. *Ibid.*

4. *Ibid.*

5. *Ibid.*, p. 125.

6. *Ibid.*, p. 127.

7. *Ibid.*, p. 128.

8. *Ibid.*

9. William Dickey, "Poem Descending a Staircase: Hypertext and the Simultaneity of Experience," in Paul Delany and George P. Landow, ed, *Hypermedia and Literary Studies* (Cambridge: MIT Press, 1991), p. 149.

10. *Ibid.*, p. 150.

11. Bill Cosford, "The Director, His Icons, His Art and His Crusade: Peter Greenaway Is Out to Redefine Film," *The Miami Herald*, December 1, 1991, Section I, p. 4.

12. Steven Levy, "Brave New World," *Rolling Stone*, June 14, 1990, p.92.

13. Woody Allen, "The Kuglemass Episode," *The New Yorker*, May 2, 1977.

14. Jay David Bolter and Michael Joyce, "Hypertext and Creative Writing," in *Hypertext '87 Proceedings*, University of North Carolina, November 13-15, 1987 (New York: Association for Computing Machinery, 1989), p. 41.

15. *Ibid.*, pp. 41-42.

16. *Ibid.*, p. 42.
17. George P. Landow and Paul Delaney, "Hypertext, Hypermedia and Literary Studies: the State of the Art," in Paul Delaney and George P. Landow, eds., *Hypermedia and Literary Studies* (Cambridge: MIT Press, 1990), p. 3.
18. *Ibid*, p. 42.
19. Carl Zimmer, "Floppy Fiction," *Discover*, November 1989, p. 34.
20. *Ibid.*, p. 36.
21. Ted Nelson, *Dream Machines* (Microsoft Press: Redmond Washington, 1987),   p.30.
22. Laurence Sterne, *The Life and Opinions of Tristram Shandy, Gentleman* (Boston: Houghton, Mifflin Co., 1965), p. 83.
23. J. David Bolter,*Writing Space: The Computer, Hypertext and the History of Writing* (Hillsdale, NJ: Lawrence Erlbaum Associates, 1991), p. 134.
24. Bolter, *Writing Space*, p. 137.
25. *Ibid.*
26. Jorge Luis Borges, *Ficciones*, edited with an introduction by Anthony Kerrigan (New York: Grove Press, 1962), pp. 99 and 100. See Bolter and Joyce, "Hypertext and Creative Writing," pp. 47–48 for a description of Borges's *Ficciones* as interactive fiction. Also see Bolter, *Writing Space*, pp. 137–139. Most of my discussion in this section is drawn from these works.
27. *Ibid.*, p. 46.
28. Walter Ong, *Orality and Literacy: The Technologizing of the Word* (London: Methuen, 1982), p. 15.
29. Vernor Vinge, *True Names . . . and Other Dangers* (New York: Baen Books, 1987), p.60.
30. Ray Bradbury, *Fahrenheit 451* (New York: Ballantine Books, 1989), p. 20.
31. *Ibid.*, pp. 54–55.

Chapter 9

Cyberscholarship and the Reinvention of the University

A 1514 illustration of the scholar St. Jerome by Albrecht Durer.

The Difference Engine, with all of its components, is radically transforming higher education. Rather than being just a word-processor and efficiency tool, the computer redefines the learning and research space of colleges and universities. In the following chapter, I look at the implications of this process and its implications for scholarship and teaching, and the emergence of what I term "cyberscholarship."

Change in the Existing
Computer Environment

During the 1950s scholarship in more quantitatively oriented fields such as physics, engineering, mathematics and psychology was transformed through the use of data analysis involving mainframe computers. The use of these intellectually empowering environments was highly circumscribed. The humanities and the arts, "soft" or qualitative fields, were largely excluded from using the computers. Mainframes were for scientists, not social scientists or humanists and artists.

The microcomputer or personal computer revolution that started during the late 1970s overturned the domination of mainframe computing models that have excluded less quantitatively oriented traditions. Interested scholars, who were largely excluded from mainframe computing resources because their subjects were not considered "appropriate" or important enough, could suddenly get access to machines of their own. With new users taking advantage of the machines, new types of software (word processors, graphic programs, hypertext systems, etc.) began to be developed. This did not mean, however, that resources were redistributed equitably. In most universities across the country, computing at all levels (mainframe and personal or desktop computing) has been kept under the control of centralized mainframe computing centers. Lip service was paid to providing for less traditional computer needs, but financial and personal resources usually continued to be put into mainframe operations.

This hegemony was increasingly challenged during the 1980s and 1990s, and now well into the new century. To a large degree, the redefinition of college and university computing environments is a result of the fact that computing has become cheaper and more accessible—a function explained, at least in part, by Moore's Law. In 1964, Gordon Moore, the co-founder of the Intel Corporation, argued that the number of transistors put on electronic chips or processors would double every two years. This means that in the case of computers, computing power would double every 24 months. In fact, "Moore's Law" has been revised as chips have become more sophisticated at an ever faster rate. Now the law states that the number doubles every 18 months, meaning that computing power is currently quadrupling every three years. Translated, this means that the computers being bought today are four times more powerful than the ones purchased three years ago.

In 1987, Christopher Dede argued how a decade earlier in 1977:

> $3,500 could buy an Apple II with an eight-bit, one megahertz processor, 48
> K of RAM, eight K of ROM, a 40 character by 24-line upper-case display, high-
> resolution graphics (280 by 192, 16 colors), two 140 K disks with a controller
> and an RF Modulator to connect with a television set. Adjusting for ten years of
> inflation, an equivalent amount of buying power today is $6,800. For that price
> one can buy a MacIntosh II with a 16-megahertz 32-bit processor, one Megabyte
> of RAM, 170K of ROM, two 800 K disk drives, a 20-megabyte internal hard disk,
> and a 640 by 480 RGB Display with 256 colors.[1]

Twenty-three years later in 2010, the machine described by Dede seems
hopelessly outdated. Personal digital assistants that are carried around by
people to keep track of their appointments have more memory and power than
the typical microcomputer of the early 1990s. Video game processors such as
Microsoft's Xbox have greater power than large desktop and personal computers
from the mid 1990s. The new iPad has a one gigahertz processor and 32 gigabyte
hard drive. When compared to the device described above (a one megahertz
processor) its processor is one thousand times more powerful. Its storage capacity
is 1,664 times as large. This is for a portable device that is priced, depending
on its configuration for between $500 and $1,000. Computing is now not only
affordable and powerful, but essential to the future mission of higher education.

Colleges and universities are having to update their computing environments,
if for no other reason than the fact that it is being demanded of them by
increasingly computer literate students—students introduced to the world of
computers through hypermedia formats such as those found on computer
games and on the Internet, and as part of their education at the elementary
and secondary levels. Students entering colleges and universities are implicitly
demanding that equivalent if not superior technologies to these be used in their
classrooms. The traditional reference room in many institutions is increasingly
becoming a computer center or information commons.

Cyberscholars and the Implications
of Cyberscholarship

J. David Bolter argued in *Turing's Man* that:

> The computer is a medium of communication as well as a scientific tool, and
> it can be used by humanists as well as scientists. It brings concepts of physics,
> mathematics and logic into the humanist's world as no previous machine has
> done. Yet it can also serve to carry artistic and philosophical thinking into the
> scientific community.[2]

The use of the computer in its manifestation as the Difference Engine has the potential to not only integrate fields of academic inquiry, but also to create major new lines of research and new methods of teaching. A new type of scholarship and instruction is emerging—one which will represent a significant challenge to older models. The term I have invented to define this phenomenon is *cyberscholarship*, and the individuals engaged in its pursuit *cyberscholars*.

My use of the term cyberscholarship is based on the word cybernetics, which was originally coined by Norbert Wiener who derived the word from the Greek word *kubernnetes* or "steersman."[3] Cyberscholarship literally involves new ways of steering oneself through the collection of knowledge and the process of inquiry.

How will the process of scholarly inquiry and teaching potentially be redefined by the various models and technologies that are part of the emerging phenomenon of cyberscholarship? In the following section I will provide some examples through the examination of one of these technologies—i.e., hypertext and hypermedia.

New Models of Scholarship and Teaching

In the past, the development of scholarly concordances—i.e. indexes of subjects and topics—has been a time-consuming and extremely difficult process. Using computer technologies that are components of the Difference Engine makes it possible to create such concordances almost automatically as part of the compilation of texts. For example, suppose that a scholar wants to determine how often the word "God" is used in the *Old Testament*, and whether or not its use is different or the same each time it appears. A relatively simple search function, like that used in most word processing systems, makes the isolation of the word's use extremely easy. Further tools can be used to compare the length of sentences, contextual variables and other factors related to the use of the word. While such technologies were available on a limited basis in mainframe computer environments, their widespread use has developed largely as a result of the technologies that constitute the Difference Engine.

On the Internet, for example, Project Gutenberg (http://promo.net/pg/), as well as other online electronic text projects, are creating massive searchable files of thousands of classic literary texts from Shakespeare to Tolstoy. New uses are only limited by the scope of one's imagination. Suppose that you are a teacher interested in showing Shakespeare's use of simile to your students. By accessing an electronic text of all of his plays and poetry you can enter a global search for the word "like" and find thousands of examples of his use of metaphors and similes in his writing. In a similar fashion, you can search out his individual use of specific words.

A search of the word *like*, for example, in Mark Twain's *The Adventures of Huckleberry Finn* brings to light the two following quotes:

> But Tom, he WAS so proud and joyful, he just COULDN'T hold in, and his
> tongue just WENT it—she a-chipping in, and spitting fire all along, and both of
> them going it at once, like a cat convention;

> Tom rose square up in bed, with his eye hot, and his nostrils opening and
> shutting like gills,

One could conceivably search out words, or references to specific characters or
historical events, depending on one's interest. A researcher could do this for
virtually any text in almost any field, as long as a digital text source (on or offline)
was available to search.

Traditional academic publishing is transformed by the Difference Engine.
James J. O'Donnell, for example, believes that computerization is radically redefining the nature of scholarly publishing. According to him:

> The reigning monarch of scholarly publication, however—the eminent
> monograph from a distinguished press—is in serious jeopardy. The traditional
> monograph, with its sustained linear argument, its extraordinarily high costs
> of publication and distribution, and its numerous inefficiencies of access, is
> beginning to look more and more like a great lumbering dinosaur.[4]

New types of publishing models will be introduced—are in fact already
transforming library collections. In the future publishing and books will reside
as a result of the Difference Engine primarily in cyberspace. One need only to see
the decline of traditional print based encyclopedias such as *Britannica* and their
substitution by online royalty-free products such as *Wikipedia* to understand the
extent to which this is the case.

This transformation is also clearly at work with archival collections. Easy and
rapid access to online archives has been redefining traditional scholarship for
at least a decade now. Comparisons, which from a practical point of view were
impossible to explore, become practical and convenient to pursue. Take, for
example, a hypertext system based around the great photographs taken during
the American Depression by the Farm Security Administration. Approximately
112,000 of these images in black and white are currently available from the
Library of Congress American Memory Project (http://memory.loc.gov/
ammem/) on the World Wide Web. A smaller collection of approximately
1,600 Farm Security Administration photographs taken in color between 1938
and 1944 are also available through the Library of Congress (http://memory.
loc.gov/ammem/fsowhome.html).

A sophisticated search system makes it possible to examine these photographs
according to the state or territory where they were photographed, their subject,
their photographer and the date when they were taken. Using the American
Memory Project's search engine you can ask the system to search for subjects

and collections that would not otherwise be feasible to pursue. Suppose, for example, that you wanted to look at all of the photographs that deal with racial discrimination in movie theaters that were taken by the FSA during the 1930s and 1940s. The system's search program can select "movie theaters," and if properly indexed "racial discrimination" and list these images in chronological order with their catalog numbers and captions. This is a very easy task that can be accomplished literally in seconds, that would take weeks to do if you had access to the necessary indexes and microfilm collections, or if you wished to search, photo by photo, through those files at the Library of Congress.

Belzoni, Mississippi, in the delta area. October 1939. Marion Post Wolcott, photographer. "Negro man entering movie theater by 'Colored' entrance." [Signs: "Colored—Adm." and "White Men Only."] Courtesy of the Library of Congress.

In the sciences, computer modeling has made it possible to conduct tasks that would otherwise be impossible. In the early 1990s, for example, using digitally constructed hypermedia images, Ping-Kang Hsuing and Robert H. P. Dunn created visual simulations of what an object would look like if moving at or near the speed of light. Using a computer program they call REST-frame, Hsiung and Dunn have created a number of images including a cubic lattice, which when stopped looks like an assembly of Tinkertoys. When accelerated to 0.99 times the speed of light, the edges of the image appear to recede and the straight rods appear to become distorted. As the lattice comes closer, the image becomes even more distorted.[5]

More recently, researchers at the University of Tübingen and Stuttgart have created images of the planet Saturn from the viewpoint of a spaceship moving at slightly less than the speed of light. This and other images are intended to provide researchers and students with the means by which to visualize Special and General Relativity (http://www.tat.physik.uni-tuebingen.de/~weiskopf/index.html).

The accurate simulation of the type described above will not only provide students and scholars with the means by which to more accurately visualize phenomena they are dealing with on a theoretical level, but will also help them better understand objects they might observe in nature. An astrophysicist familiar with a hypermedia simulation of the type described above may find it much easier to interpret the movement of celestial objects moving near the speed of light around an object such as a black hole.[6]

In areas such as biochemistry, the use of computer based molecular models and simulations has become an essential tool for the field. Research in the field is absolutely dependent upon the use of computer/simulation techniques. Without them, the field as it currently functions would not exist. The Human Genome Project—perhaps the most important collaborative scientific project of recent years—would not have been possible without the technologies provided by the Difference Engine.

Likeness, Analogy, and Metaphor

The examples included in this chapter have certain elements in common. To begin with, each makes important use of *likeness* and *analogy*. In the case of the text search for the word "God" in the Old Testament, and whether or not its use is different or the same across the document, we are trying to determine likenesses. In the case of the simulated photographs of a cubic lattice approaching the speed of light, the scientist is provided a simulated image or model that he or she can compare for likeness with actual phenomenon observable in Nature.

Metaphor, "*that which allows us to replace one kind of thought with another*,"[7] also plays a key role in the hypertext and hypermedia phenomenon. In this context, Marvin Minsky's comments on the importance of good metaphors are revealing.

> Good metaphors are useful because they transport uniframes, intact, from one world into another. Such cross-realm correspondences can enable us to transport entire families of problems into other realms, in which we can apply to them some already well-developed skills.[8]

On one level, hypertext and hypermedia systems, are tools that allow scholars to amass the memories and collections of our culture, and in turn to create new metaphors and ways of knowing—i.e., transporting "uniframes" and "entire families of problems into other realms."

I believe that the components of the Difference Engine such as hypertext and hypermedia, as well the Internet and the World Wide Web, represent tools for the magnification and extension of ideas that are as important as the telescope was to the astronomer and the microscope to the biologist in the seventeenth century. Such technologies not only transformed their fields, but also created a new human environment. This point was made quite clearly nearly forty years ago by Marshall McLuhan who argued that technological environments "are not merely passive containers of people but are active processes that reshape people and other technologies alike."[9]

The introduction of printing in the fifteenth century, as pointed out by McLuhan, played an important role in instituting new patterns of culture and scholarship throughout Europe.[10] The Difference Engine has the potential to do the same in our own era. It is already clear that these and related computer technologies will create not only new sources of information and new methods of analyzing data, but new ways of conceptualizing and symbolically constructing the world. New standards of scholarship will emerge, because new standards are possible. Likewise, new questions and debates will arise because the tools necessary to set the stage for such debates will be available. As J. David Bolter argues, the

> humanist will not be able to ignore the medium with which he too will work daily: it will shape his thought in subtle ways, suggest possibilities, and impose limitations, as does any other medium of communication. . . . The scientist or philosopher who works with such electronic tools will think in different ways from those who have worked at ordinary desks with paper and pencil, with stylus and parchment, or with papyrus. He will choose different problems and be satisfied with different solutions.[11]

In essence, the use of hypertext and hypermedia systems transforms traditional scholarship and knowledge into a much more dynamic, analogic, metaphoric, comparative and encyclopedic process. The ways in which universities and colleges train students will have to be transformed as well.

The Difference Engine as a "Singularity"

The potential transformation of scholarship in our own era that is resulting from the technologies of the Difference Engine, is similar to the same type of change as that which was experienced as a result of the introduction of printing during the Renaissance. The revolution resulting from the emergence of the Difference Engine, which parallels the transitions or shift during the Renaissance from a typographic to post-typographic culture, represents what the science fiction writer Vernor Vinge has described as a singularity:

When a race succeeds in making creatures that are smarter than it is, then all the rules are changed. And from the standpoint of that race, you've gone through a Singularity. That's because it's not possible before that point to talk meaningfully about the issues that are important *after* that point.[12]

Vinge believes that if we can use a technology to increase or create intelligence, "then we have made a fundamental change in the rules of the game, as important as our original rise to sentience."[13]

The computer technologies that represent the Difference Engine such as the Internet and World Wide Web, hypermedia, and virtual reality, represent as a combined force a singularity as defined by Vinge. Their introduction, along with related technologies such as computer simulation, and even e-mail, represents a fundamental change in the rules of scholarship. This point has been made in a more general context about the computer by Heinz Pagels in his book *The Dreams of Reason*. Pagels argues that the computer is altering the "architectonic of the sciences and the picture we have of material reality."[14]

The computer, with its ability to manage enormous amounts of data and to create simulations of reality, provides a new instrument with which to view reality. Unlike the telescope or the microscope which were analytic and produced a reductionist view of the universe, the computer produces a new class of analysis and intellectual knowledge that is essentially analogical and comparative. Examples include the previously discussed digitally constructed simulations of what objects would look like moving at or near the speed of light.

According to Pagels, the computer creates not only a new class of people struggling for intellectual and social acceptance, but "a new way of thinking about knowledge."[15] It is his belief that as a research instrument, the computer will have its initial impact on a "vertical" level by deepening our understanding of existing problems:

> Using computers, physicists, chemists, and economists can tackle problems that they could not touch before simply because the computational power was not there.[16]

Pagels feels that this ability of the computer to manage enormous amounts of information will likewise provide for fields such as economics, political science and social psychology new aspects of social reality.[17] On a "horizontal" level Pagels believes that the computer will be able to show unexpected connections between the sciences that will restructure our understanding of reality.[18]

Pagels talks about the computer as the primary instrument for understanding "the sciences of complexity." He argues that this is done by the computer's capacity to model and simulate complex systems. In fact, drawing on the work of the Peter Lax, a mathematician at the Courant Institute at New York University, Pagels maintains that the two traditional branches of knowledge—

the experimental and the theoretical—have been joined by a third branch, the computational.[19]

Traditional experiments correspond to analogical demonstrations of theory. Computational simulations correspond to digital demonstrations. According to Pagels:

> One of the ways that future science will progress is by a combination of precise observations of actual systems followed by computer modeling of those systems. This differs from the traditional notion of experimentation in which one actively alters the conditions of the actual system to try and determine what is going on.[20]

These simulations can model the behavior of a star or of a social or cultural group.

In summary, the new technologies available as part of the Difference Engine almost certainly represent singularities that transform the meaning of traditional scholarship, ways of knowing and ways of teaching. Combined together they probably represent a revolution as significant as the introduction of moveable type and the modern printed book into Western culture during the early years of the Renaissance.

The Creation of the New Knowledge Space Brings with It the Reinvention of the University

In earlier chapters we discussed the ideas of Douglas Engelbart and Levy about computers being cognition enhancers and communication devices for creating a Collective IQ. If their ideas are valid, then the university, as the principal knowledge center in our culture, is radically transformed. In point of fact, this process of transformation is already well underway. Knowledge (not necessarily wisdom) is evolving at an unprecedented speed. The numbers of people being taught are larger than at any point in our history, and the tools with which we are using to extend our knowledge and communicate it with one another are unlike anything we have thus far experienced.

In this context, it is useful to look at Pierre Levy's concept of the cosmopedia and more specifically his definition of "collective intelligence." For Levy, collective intelligence "is a form of *univerally distributed intelligence*, constantly enhanced, coordinated in real time, and resulting in the effective mobilization of skills."[21] We move from the Cartesian notion of *cogito* (I think) to *cogitus* (we think).[22]

The invention of a new knowledge space—one based around the creation of a collective intelligence—represents a paradigm shift in our thinking about universities, information processing, scholarship and teaching. Mainframe and desktop computers will continue to be used, but the assumptions underlying their function and operation will have little or no meaning in the traditional ways they have been used up until now. Instead, models of collective intelligence will supersede the limited function of the computer as just an information processor.

For higher education this means rethinking where computing is housed in the university and how it functions. Historically, computers have been the domain of engineers and programmers. Should the people who create machines necessarily dictate how they are used? I would argue that the computer and its various iterations in terms of hypertext, hypermedia, the Internet, the Web and virtual reality, represents a territory best understood by philosophers rather than programmers, social theorists rather bureaucrats, and poets rather than technical writers. This shift represents what I refer to as "digital rhetoric." As a phenomenon it is distinctly post-modern.

Digital Rhetoric

Traditionally rhetoric has been defined as either the study of schemes and tropes—ones involving verbal artifice—or as the study of persuasion. Rhetoric is viewed with suspicion by most members of the academy. Going back to the Renaissance, it has been argued that reason should rule over imagination—language rather than being rhetorical should be either scientific, expository or philosophical.

Richard Lanham has argued with remarkable insight in his book *The Electronic Word: Democracy, Technology, and the Arts* that:

> In the digital light of these technologies, the disciplinary boundaries that currently govern academic study of the arts dissolve before our eyes, as do the administrative structures that enshrine them. It is not only the distinction between the creator and the critic that dissolves, but the walls between painting and music and sculpture, music, architecture, and literature.[23]

For Lanham the electronic text and by association the Difference Engine, "not only creates a new writing space, but a new educational space as well."[24] The computer frames inquiry differently than the printed book. As a rhetorical device, it allows thinking to occur in very specific ways—ones that potentially challenge older traditions. The traditional Western literary canon, for example, has been under considerable challenge in recent years as other literatures and cultures have been brought to light which question its dominance.

New configurations of text such as those made possible through hypertext changes the rhetoric of reading—whether from the traditional literary canon or any other source. Through the machinery and digital logic of the computer, the text no longer stands as absolute and authoritative, but deeply cultural, created at a specific moment in time, culturally influenced, politically shaped and linked to specific values and world views.

As we have seen in earlier chapters, hypertext, and the computer technology that underlies it, has the potential to deconstruct the text—to show its secondary and tertiary meanings, its true sources and origins. In doing so it changes the very nature of scholarship and inquiry, and ultimately the nature and character of the university. As Lanham explains, the shift from the print to the electronic screen, leads to a condition in which:

> The fixed printed surface become volatile and interactive. The definitive and unchange-able text upon which Western humanism has been based since the Renaissance, and the Arnoldian "masterpeice" theory of culture built upon it, are called into question.[25]

The computer as a mediating force allows the creation of a new digital rhetoric. According to Lanham, "digitalization has made the arts interchangeable."[26] A visual sign can be transformed into a musical representation, a letter can be zoomed in on until it changes from an alphabetic sign into a pixillated abstract form on the computer screen.[27]

The educational order, the structure and meaning of knowledge and the university are redefined by the new digital rhetoric. What happens to Chaucer's *Canterbury Tales* when read on the computer screen? Using multimedia the text can be read aloud and heard in Middle English and properly pronounced as the author originally intended it. Lanham explains how as an English teacher rather than trying to diagram the Great Vowel Shift on the blackboard, he can now potentially "explain the vowel shift through a computer-graphics program that put sight, sound and phonological history together."[28]

Much of the expertise, and power of university professors is a result of the authority they have as a result of their expertise in a particular subject. In large part this is a result of their having mastered large sources of data—sources of data not easily accessible to the general population or even advanced students. What happens when this information becomes more easily available through sources like the Internet?

Likewise what happens when discourse occurs, at least in part, in an online context. Lanham, for example, argues that in a university classroom using net-worked computers the professor becomes one of many potential voices online. Voices that are normally too timid to speak out may be encouraged to reveal themselves in the computer mediated space of the online discussion.[29]

In other areas the digital rhetoric of the computer transforms the way we interpret texts or materials we consider ourselves very familiar with. Robert Winter in his widely acclaimed and pioneering multimedia program the *Ninth Symphony*, not only presented an interesting reexamination of Beethoven's work, but a new model of digital rhetoric and instruction. Although I have always loved Beethoven's work, I am not a musician and have had very little understanding of how the various themes and parts of the *Ninth* were interrelated. Through the use of Winter's program, his "repurposing" of existing performances and his examination of the deep structure of the piece, I began to understand the piece at a new level. Being able to read the text of the choral section in the 4th movement, being in fact able to participate in the chorus, to see the structure and logic of the music, was a transforming and new type of learning experience.

As was the case with the introduction of book culture during the Renaissance, profound dysfunctions between the old and new models of scholarship and teaching will undoubtedly develop. It seems unavoidable that the emergence of the new paradigm will probably be met with a great deal of enthusiasm or skepticism depending upon which camp an individual chooses. The eventual dominance of a new—and yet largely undetermined—paradigm, however, seems almost certain.

*   *   *

In all of this, the question arises as to what happens to colleges and universities, their traditions of scholarship and teaching? The emergence of new models of digital rhetoric, augmented and collective intelligence, and cyberscholarship as part of the creation of the Difference Engine raises important questions for educators. How do we train students to meet the new models of scholarship? How will the rules of academic politics change? In what ways does it seem likely that the nature and character of college and university scholarship and teaching will change in years to come?

Notes

1. Christopher J. Dede, "Empowering Environments, Hypermedia and Microworlds," *The Computing Teacher*, November 1987, p. 20.

2. J. David Bolter, *Turing's Man: Western Culture in the Computer Age* (Chapel Hill: University of North Carolina Press, 1984), p. xi.

3. Norbert Wiener, *The Human Use of Human Beings: Cybernetics and Society* (New York: Avon Books, 1967), p. 24. Also see: Wiener, *Cybernetics, or Control and Communication in the Animal and the Machine*, 2nd ed. (Cambridge, Mass: MIT Press, 1961).

4. James J. O'Donnell, *Avatars of the Word: From Papyrus to Cyberspace* (Cambridge: Harvard University Press, 1998), p. 58.

5. Ivars Peterson, "Space-Time Odyssey: Visualizing the Effects of Traveling Near the Speed of Light," *Science News*, Vol. 137 (April 14, 1990), 232.

6. *Ibid.*, p. 233.

7. Marvin Minsky, *The Society of Mind* (New York: Simon & Schuster, 1986), p. 298.

8. *Ibid.*, p. 299.

9. Marshall McLuhan, *The Gutenberg Galaxy: The Making of Typographic Man* (Toronto: University of Toronto Press, 1962), page preceding prologue, p. 1.

10. *Ibid.*, p. 12.

11. Bolter, *Turing's Man*, pp. 6-8.

12. Vernor Vinge, "Hurtling Towards the Singularity," interview with Michael Synergy, *Mondo 2000* (1989), p. 116.

13. Vernor Vinge, *True Names . . . and Other Dangers* (New York: Simon & Schuster, 1987), p. 1.

14. Heinz R. Pagels, *The Dreams of Reason: The Computer and the Rise of the Sciences of Complexity* (New York: Bantam Books, 1989), p. 13.

15. *Ibid*, pp. 13-14.

16. *Ibid.*, p. 41.

17. *Ibid.*, p. 42.

18.. *Ibid.*, p. 42.

19. *Ibid.*, pp. 42-43.

20. *Ibid.*, p. 43.

21. *Ibid*, p. 13.

22. *Ibid*, p. 17.

23. Richard A. Lanham, *The Electronic Word: Democracy, Technology, and the Arts* (Chicago: University of Chicago Press, 1993), p. 13.

24. *Ibid*, p. xii.

25. Lanham, p. 73.

26. *Ibid*, p. 130.

27. *Ibid*, p. 132.

28. *Ibid*.

29. *Ibid*, p. 79.

Chapter 10

Conclusion:
Ideal Speech and the Difference
Engine

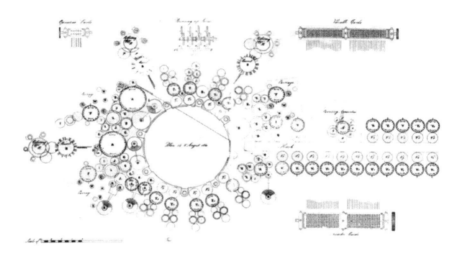

Detail from Charles Babbage's 1840 design for the Analytical Engine.

This work assumes that the different components of the Difference Engine represent a revolution in information processing—a critical phase in the emergence of a post-typographic or post-modern culture. If this is indeed the case, then the new technology has profound implications for the meaning of knowledge and literacy in our culture.

We are, in fact, at a crossroads in the definition of our culture—a profound moment in the formation of our culture. In this context, C. A. Bowers asks: "*What stories, languages, and ways of knowing do the technologists want to make the dominant feature of mainstream culture and what is the nature of subjectivity their form of culture will help constitute as the natural attitude toward everyday life?*"[1] What stories, language systems and ways of knowing are created for our culture through the use of the Difference Engine? What freedoms and restrictions are we provided through its use? In answering these questions, we will draw on the theoretical work of Jurgen Habermas.

The Difference Engine and Ideal Speech

Jurgen Habermas has proposed a "theory of communicative action" whose main principal is what he terms "the ideal speech situation." In the ideal speech situation, all of those participating have equal power, attempt to reach understanding, do not attempt to manipulate a situation, and understand their obligation to offer reasons. In the ideal speech situation "the unforced force of the better argument" ultimately determines the outcome of things.[2]

This is a powerful philosophy and can inform our articulation of a critical theory of educational computing—one that takes into account the mechanisms implied in the Difference Engine.

To begin with: **Can hypertext and hypermedia contribute to the creation of an ideal speech situation?** I would argue yes, as a result of hypertext and hypermedia's capacity to deconstruct a text and its content and to point the reader toward the underlying assumptions and true meaning of a document, whether it is a textbook, a poem, a film or virtually any other source.

Can the augmentation of intelligence and cognition contribute to the creation of an ideal speech situation? Yes, if it contributes to our capacity to think about and organize ideas, and to function in rational and meaningful ways that best serve humankind.

Can the Internet and the World Wide Web contribute to the creation of an ideal speech situation? Yes, if used to promote understanding, the exchange of ideas and the stimulation of true dialogue. If the Internet and the World Wide Web are only used to limit and isolate the individual by encouraging her or him to avoid discourse, then its liberating function is lost.

Can collective intelligence contribute to the creation of an ideal speech situation? The answer is almost certainly yes, if collective activity can provide us the means for not only creating greater dialogue, but by combining the best of thoughts and ideas into a single unified set of arguments and conclusions.

Can simulation and hyperreality contribute to the creation of an ideal speech situation? The answer is almost certainly no. The simulation by its very nature tends to distort reality. If a simulation is used to clarify or explicate some from of knowledge, it should be created with the greatest care and skepticism on the part of these engaged in the simulation.

Can the panoptic sort contribute to the creation of an ideal speech situation? Almost certainly not. The panoptic sort, by its very nature, contradicts Habermas's requirement that the ideal speech situation gives all of those participating in a dialogue equal power and that manipulation is not allowed. This is contradicted by the essentially unequal nature of the panoptic sort, which gives one individual power over another through their control of information.

Unfortunately, there has been almost no discussion by the leaders of educational computing or in their writings and research, of any of the cultural or social meanings of the new technology. Other than Bowers, and a few others, there seems to be no understanding that educational computing and technology is deeply cultural, and that we must develop a critical philosophy of educational computing.

This work is an effort in this direction. By explicating the realities of the "Difference Engine" and its emergence as an increasingly powerful force in our culture and educational system, the first step toward addressing its severe limitations can be taken.

Can the increasingly widespread use of mobile computing contribute to the creation of an ideal speech situation? The answer is yes, if in using this technology we do not become so distracted that we no longer engage in authentic ways with people in the real world. We are social creatures who exist in social spaces, and mobile technology can distract us from the immediate aspects of ours lives. Mobile computing can clearly contribute to an ideal speech situation, but only if used in certain ways.

Conclusion

Once again, we return to the work of C. A. Bowers. As Bowers argues about educational computing in general, the elements that constitute the "Difference Engine" (i.e., *Hypertext/Hypermedia, Augmented Cognition and Intelligence, Networked Information and Communication Systems, Collective Intelligence, Hyperreality,* the *Panoptic Sort* and *Mobile Computing,* must be understood in terms of what they select for *amplification* and *reduction.*

As discussed in the previous pages, the Difference Engine is not a neutral technology, but instead, a specific value-laden means of constructing and knowing the world. The creation of the Difference Engine is by no means complete and will continue for years to come. The recent remarkable growth of the Internet, particularly through the introduction of the World Wide Web, is a clear demonstration of this point. New parts and functions will continue to be added to "the engine."

The Difference Engine is by definition a machine that is constantly evolving. It must be understood in the context of the cultural orientations that it reinforces.[3] As such, it needs to be understood as:

> an integral part of a complex ecology that includes both the cultural and natural environment. This cultural pattern of thinking works, in a sense, like lenses that enable us to see certain entities while putting other aspects out of focus. When we think that expertise in the area of computers involves only a technical form of knowledge for using and improving computers, we are, in fact, under the influence of the conceptual guidance system of our culture. In terms of the cultural bias built into our way of thinking, new ideas and technologies are understood as progressive by their very nature. But what is not as clearly recognized is that the new forms of knowledge and technologies often lead to unanticipated consequences whose disruption may outweigh any gains from the innovations.[4]

Like Prospero in Shakespeare's *The Tempest*, we must come to terms with a "brave new world," one that has been reinvented through the introduction of radical new technologies such as those that make up the "Difference Engine." Traditional studies in the computer field unfortunately do not provide adequate grounding to fully understand what computer systems such as the ones I have outlined in this book mean in the context of human practice and education.[5]

The Difference Engine gives us "new freedoms" and "new dependencies."[6] Increasingly, we need to be aware that technologies such as the computer have the potential, if we do not employ their use carefully, to dehumanize us by separating us from nature and from our human selves. This is already happening in a number of different ways—some that do not include computers. As Joseph Weizenbaum has argued in reference to the biofeedback movement: "man no longer even senses himself, his body, directly, but only through pointer readings, flashing lights, and buzzing sounds produced by instruments attached to him as speedometers, are attached to automobiles."[7]

As we have argued throughout this work, computers in the form of the Difference Engine, have the potential to transform our culture in revolutionary ways. But we must not allow these machines and systems to diminish or reduce our humanity. As we enter the early stages in the development and use of this remarkable technology, we must also be aware of its limitations and its potential to distort and control us. Based on our previous adaptation of other technologies, I am not convinced that we will necessarily make the best and most effective use of this new technology. This is unfortunate in light of the new technology's potential to expand our awareness and better realize our human potential.

We need to heed the warning of Winograd and Flores and "step back and examine the implicit understanding of design that guides technological development within our existing tradition of thought."[8] Only by doing so can we begin to realize the possibilities and alternatives open to us through the new computer technologies without, at the same time, alienating ourselves from our own innermost feelings and sensations as well as from the world around us.

Only through a critical understanding of computers, of their cultural meaning and educational meaning, can we have any hope of achieving the elements of Habermas's situation of ideal speech. It is hoped that this work represents a step in moving our educational system and culture in that direction.

Notes

1. C. A. Bowers, *Educating for an Ecologically Sustainable Culture: Rethinking Moral Education, Creativity, Intelligence and Other Modern Orthodoxies* (Albany: State University of New York Press, 1995), p. 83.

2. Jurgen Habermas, *Communication and the Evolution of Society* (London: Heinnemann Educational Books, 1979). Note particularly Chapters 1-2. For a discussion of the Ideal Speech Situation in an educational context, see: Robert Young, *A Critical Theory of Education: Habermas and Our Children's Future* (New York: Teachers College Press, 1990), pp. 75-78, 99-100, 126-127.

3. C. A. Bowers, *The Cultural Dimensions of Educational Computing* (New York: Teachers College Press, 1988), p. 7.

4. *Ibid.*, p. 2.

5. Terry Winograd and Fernando Flores, *Understanding Computers and Cognition* (Massachusetts: Addison-Wesley Publishing Company, 1987), p. 4.

6. Stewart Brand, *The Media Lab: Inventing the Future at M.I.T.* (New York: Penguin Books, 1988), p. 256.

7. Joseph Weizenbaum, *Computer Power and Human Reason* (San Francisco: W. H. Freeman and Company, 1976), p. 259.

8. Winograd and Flores, p. 5.

Bibliography

Adler, Mortimer. *The Great Ideas: A Synopticon of Great Books of the Western World.* Chicago: Encyclopedia Britannica, Inc., 1952.

Allen, Woody. "The Kugelmas Episode." *The New Yorker,* May 2, 1977.

Alter, Jonathan. "When Photographs Lie." *Newsweek,* July 30, 1990: 44-46.

Ambron, Sueann, and Kristina Hooper, eds. *Interactive Multimedia: Visions of Multimendia for Developers, Educators, and Information Providers.* Redmond, WA: Microsoft Press, 1988.

Barrett, Edward, ed. *The Society of the Text: Hypertext, Hypermedia and The Social Construction of Information.* Cambridge, MA: MIT Press, 1989.

——. ed. *Text, ConText, and Hypertext: Writing with and for the Computer.* Cambridge, MA: MIT Press, 1988.

Bascomb, Anne W. "Who Owns Creativity?" In Tom Forester, ed., *Computers in the Human Context.* Cambridge, MA: MIT Press, 1989, 407-414.

Baudrillard, Jean. *Selected Writings,* edited by Mark Poster. Stanford, CA: Stanford University Press, 1988.

——. *Simulations.* Translated by Paul Foos, Paul Patton and Phillip Beitchman. New York: Semiotext(e), 1983.

Becker, Ernest. *The Structure of Evil.* New York: Free Press, 1978.

Benedikt, Michael. *Cyberspace: First Steps.* Cambridge, MA: MIT Press, 1992.

Beniger, James R. *The Control Revolution: Technological and Economic Origins of the Information Society.* Cambridge, MA: Harvard University Press, 1986.

Bentham, Jeremy. *Panopticon; or, the Inspection-House: Containing the Idea of a New Principle of Construction Applicable to Any Sort of Establishment, In Which Persons of Any Description Are to be Kept Under Inspection: And in Particular to Penitentiary-Houses, Prisons, Poor Houses, Lazarettos, Houses of Industry, Manufactories, Hospitals, Work-Houses, Mad-Houses, and Schools: With a Plan of Management Adapted to the Principles: In a Series of Letters, Written in the Year 1787, from Crecheff in White Russia, To a Friend in England, Included in The Works of Jeremy Bentham.* Volume Four, John Bowring, ed. New York: Russell & Russell, Inc., 1962.

Berners-Lee, Tim (with Mark Fischitti). *Weaving the Web : The Original Design and Ultimate Destiny of the World Wide Web by Its Iinventor.* San Francisco: HarperSanFrancisco, 1999.

Birkerts, Sven. *The Gutenberg Elegies: The Fate of Reading in an Electronic Age.* Boston: Faber and Faber, 1994.

Black, John B., Karen Swan and Daniel L. Schwartz. "Developing Thinking Skills With Computers." *Teachers College Record,* 89, 3 (Spring 1988): 384-407.

Bogard, William. "Sociology in the Absence of the Social: The Significance of Baudrillard for Contemporary Thought." *Philosophy and Social Criticism* 13, 3 (1987): 227-242.

Bolter, J. David. *Turing's Man: Western Culture in the Computer Age.* Chapel Hill: University of North Carolina Press, 1984.

——. *Writing Space: The Computer, Hypertext and the History of Writing* Hillsdale, NJ: Lawrence Erlbaum, 1991.

Bolter, J. David, and Michael Joyce. "Hypertext and Creative Writing." In *Hypertext '87 Proceedings.* New York: The Association for Computing Machinery, 1989.

Borges, Jorge Luis. *Ficciones.* Ed. ith an introduction by Anthony Kerrigan. NeW York: Grove Press, 1962.

Borgman, Christine M. *From Gutenberg to the Global Information Infrastructure: Access to Information in the Networked World.* Cambridge, MA: MIT Press, 2000.

Bosco, James. "The Organization of Schools and the Use of Computers to Improve Schooling." *Peabody Journal of Education* 64, 1 (Spring 1989).

Bowers, C. A. *Let Them Eat Data: How Computers Affect Education, Cultural Diversity, and the Prospects of Ecological Sustainability.* Athens: University of Georgia Press, 2000.

——. *Educating for an Ecologically Sustainable Culture: Rethinking Moral Education, Creativity, Intelligence and Other Modern Orthodoxies.* Albany: State University of New York Press, 1995.

——. *The Cultural Dimensions of Educational Computing: Understanding the NonNeutrality of Technology.* New York: Teachers College Press, 1980.

Bradbury, Ray. *Farenheit 451.* New York: Ballantine Books, 1989.

Brand, Stewart. *The Media Lab: Inventing the Future at M.I.T.* New York: Penguin Books, 1988.

——. *Two Cybernetic Frontiers.* New York: Random House, 1974.

Brin, David. *The Transparent Society: Will Technology Force Us to Choose Between Privacy and Freedom.* Reading, MA: Perseus Books, 1998.

Bromley, Hank, and Michael W. Apple. *Education/Technology/Power: Educational Computing as Social Practice.* Albany: State University of New York Press, 1998.

Bronowski, Jacob. *The Ascent of Man.* Boston: Little Brown, 1973.

Burbules, Nicholas C. "Tootle: A Parable of Schooling and Destiny." *Harvard Educational Review.* 56, 3 (August 1986): 239-256.

Burbules, Nicholas C., and Bertram C. Bruce. "This is Not a Paper." *Educational Researcher.* 24; 8 (November 1995): 12-18.

Bush, Vannevar. "As We May Think." *Atlantic Monthly* 176, 1 (1945): 101-108. Reprinted in part in Nelson's *Literary Machines,* 1/39-1/54. A full reprint of the article can be found in Irene Greif, ed., *Computer-Supported Cooperative Work,* 17-34.

Butler, Samuel. *Erewhon.* New York: Airmont, 1967.

Carr, Clay. "Hypertext: A New Training Tool." *Educational Technology.* August 1988, 7-11.

——. "Making the Human Computer Marriage Work." *Training and Development Journal.* May 1988, 65-74.

Chaiklin, Seth, and Matthew W. Lewis. "Will There Be Teachers in the Classroom of the Future? . . . . But We Don't Think about That." *Teachers College Record* 89,3 (Spring 1988): 431-440.

Chardak, Burt. "Domino's Pizza Plans a "Big Brother" Act." *Miami Herald.* September 10, 1989.

Comenius, Jan Amos. *Orbis Sensualium Pictus.* Translated by Charles Hoole. London: S. Kirton, 1659.

Conklin, Jeff. "Hypertext: An Introduction and Survey." *Computer* 20, 9 (1987): 17-41.

Cosford, Bill. "The Director, His Icons, His Art and His Crusade: Peter Greenaway Is Out to Redefine Film." *The Miami Herald.* December 1, 1991.

Crampton, Gertrude, with pictures by Tibor Gergely. *Tootle.* Racine, WI: Western Publishing, 1945.

Critical Arts Ensemble. *The Electronic Disturbance.* New York: Automedia, 1994.

Cuban, Larry. *Teachers and Machines: The Classroom Use of Technology Since 1920.* New York: Teachers College Press, 1986.

Davis, Ben. "Image Learning: Higher Education and Interactive Video Disk." *Teachers College Record.* 89, 3 (Spring 1988): 352-359.

Davis, Bennett. "Grand Illusions." *Discover,* June 1990.

Dede, Christopher J. "Empowering Environments, Hypermedia and Microworlds." *The Computing Teacher.* November 1987, 20-24, 61.

Delany, Paul and George P. Landow, eds. *Hypermedia and Literary Studies.* Cambridge: M.I.T. Press, 1991.

Dickey, William. "Poem Descending a Staircase: Hypertext and the Simultaniety of Experience." In Paul Delany and George P. Landow, eds. *Hypermedia and Literary Studies.* Cambridge: MIT

Press, 199.

Diderot, Denis. *Encyclopedia Selections*. Translated by Nelly Hoyt and Thomas Cassirer Schwab. Indianapolis: The Bobbs-Merrill Company, Inc., 1965.

Drexler, Eric. *Engines of Creation*. New York: Doubleday, 1986.

Eco, Umberto. *Travels in Hyperreality*. Translated from the Italian by William Weaver. New York: Harcourt Brace & Company, 1990.

Eisenstein, Elizabeth. *Print Culture and Enlightenment Thought*. Chapel Hill, NC: Hanes Foundation, 1986.

——. *The Printing Revolution in Early Modern Europe*. New York: Cambridge University Press, 1983.

Englebart, Douglas. "A Conceptual Framework for the Augmentation of Man's Intellect." In P. W. Howerton and D. C. Weeks, *Vistas in Information Handling: Vol. 1. The Augmentation of Man's Intellect by Machine*. Washington, DC: Spartan Books, 1963, 1-29.

——. "Toward Augmenting the Human Intellect and Boosting our Collective I. Q.," *Communications of the ACM*, Vol. 38, 8, August 1995, p. 30.

Firme, Matthew A. "Populous." *Game Player's PC Strategy Guide*. March/April 1990: 91.

Forester, Tom, ed. *Computers in the Human Context*. Cambridge: M.I.T. Press, 1989.

Forster, E. M. *The Eternal Moment and Other Stories*. New York: Harcourt Brace, 1956.

——. "The Machine Stops." Included in *The Collected Tales of E. M. Forster*. New York: Alfred A. Knopf, 1959.

Foucault, Michel. *Discipline and Punish*. Translated by Alan Sheridan. New York: Random House, 1979.

Franz, George, and Seymour Papert. "Computer as Material: Messing About with Time." *Teachers College Record* 89, 3 (Spring 1988): 408-417.

Gandy, Oscar H. *The Panoptic Sort: A Political Economy of Personal Information*. Boulder, CO: Westview Press, 1993.

Gee, James Paul. *What Video Games Have to Teach Us About Learning and Literacy*. New York: Palgrave Macmillan, 2003.

Gerver, Elizabeth. *Humanizing Technologizing*. New York: Plenum Press, 1986.

Gibson, William. *Count Zero*. New York: Ace, 1987.

——. *Neuromancer*. New York: Ace, 1984.

Gilreath, James, and Douglas L. Wilson, eds. *Thomas Jefferson's Library: A Catalog with the Entries in His Own Order*. Washington, DC: Library of Congress, 1989.

Giroux, Henry A., Colin Lankshear, Peter McLaren and Michael Peters. *Counternarratives: Cultural Studies and Critical Pedagogies in Postmodern Spaces*. New York: Routledge, 1996.

Goffman, Erving. *Frame Analysis: An Essay on the Organization of Human Experience*. New York: Harper and Row, 1974.

Greif, Irene, ed. *Computer-Supported Cooperative Work: A Book of Readings*. San Mateo, CA: Morgan Kaufmann Publishers, Inc., 1988.

Habermas, Jurgen. *Communication and the Evolution of Society*. London: Heinnemann Educational Books, 1979.

Hardison, O. B. *Disappearing Through the Skylight: Culture and Technology in the Twentieth Century*. New York: Penguin Books, 1989.

Harrison, Teresa M., and Timothy Stephen, eds. *Computer Networking and Scholarly Communication in the Twenty-First-Century University*. New York: State University of New York Press, 1996.

Heim, Michael. *The Metaphysics of Virtual Reality*. New York: Oxford University Press, 1993.

Herbert, Frank. *Dune*. New York: Berkley Medallion Books, 1965.

Hillis, Daniel. *The Connection Machine*. Cambridge, MA: MIT, 1985.

Howard, Robert. *Brave New Workplace*. New York: Penguin Books, 1985.

Hutchins, Robert M. *The Great Conversation: The Substance of a Liberal Education*. Chicago: Encyclopedia Britannica, 1952.

Illich, Ivan. *In the Vineyard of the Text: A Commentary to Hugh's Didascalion*. Chicago: University of Chicago Press, 1993.

Jacobs, Joseph. *The Fables of Aesop*. Illustrated by Richard Heighway. New York: Schocken Books, 1964. First published in 1894.

Joyce, Michael. *Of Two Minds: Hypertext Pedagogy and Politics*. Ann Arbor: University of Michigan Press, 1995.

Kay, Alan, and Adele Goldberg. "Personal Dynamic Media." *Computer* 10 (March 1977): 31-41.

Kellner, Douglas. *Jean Baudrillard: From Marxism to Postmodernism and Beyond*. Stanford, CA: Stanford University Press, 1989.

Kuhn, Thomas. *The Structure of Scientific Revolutions*. Chicago: University of Chicago Press, 1962.

Landow, George P. "Hypertext in Literary Education, Criticism and Scholarship." *Computers in the Humanities* 23 (1989): 173.

——. *Hypertext: The Convergence of Contemporary Critical Theory and Technology*. Baltimore, MD: Johns Hopkins University Press, 1992.

——. "The Rhetoric of Hypermedia: Some Rules for Authors." *Journal of Computing in Higher Education* 1, 1 (Spring 1989).

——. ed. *Hyper/Text/Theory*. Baltimore, MD: The Johns Hopkins University Press, 1994.

Landow, George P. and Paul Delaney. "Hypertext, Hypermedia and Literary Studies: The State of the Art." In Paul Delaney and George P. Landow, eds. *Hypermedia and Literary Studies*. Cambridge: MIT Press, 19 .

Lanham, Richard, A. *The Electronic Word: Democracy, Technology and the Arts*. Chicago: University of Chicago Press, 1993.

Le Rond d'Alembert, Jean. *Preliminary Discourse to the Encyclopedia of Diderot*. Translated by R. Schwab. Indianapolis: The Bobbs-Merrill Company, Inc., 1963.

Lévy, Pierre. *Collective Intelligence: Mankind's Emerging World in Cyberspace*. Translated by Robert Bononno. New York: Plenum, 1997.

Levy, Steven. "Brave New World." *Rolling Stone*, June 14, 1990.

——. *Hackers: Heroes of the Computer Revolution*. New York: Dell, 1984.

——. "People and Computers in Commerce: A Spreadsheet Way of Knowledge." In Tom Forester, ed. *Computers in the Human Context*. Cambridge, MA: MIT Press, 1989, 318-326.

Luke, Timothy W. "Touring Hyperreality: Critical Theory Confronts Informational Society." In Philip Wexler, ed. *Critical Theory Now*. London: Falmer Press, 1991, 1-26.

Lunenfeld, Peter, ed. *The Digital Dialectic: New Essays on New Media*. Cambridge: MIT Press, 2000.

Lyon, David. *The Electronic Eye: The Rise of the Surveillance Society*. Minneapolis: University of Minnesota Press, 1994.

Lyotard, Jean-Francois. "Answering the Question: What is Postmodernism?" Included in Charles Jencks, ed. *The Post-Modern Reader*. New York: St. Martin's Press, 1992.

——. *La Condition Postmoderne: Rapport Sur le Savoir*. Paris: Les Editions de Minuit, 1979.

McClintock, Robert O. "Marking the Second Frontier." *Teachers College Record* 89, 3 (Spring 1988): 345-351.

McLuhan, Marshall. *The Gutenberg Galaxy: The Making of Typographic Man*. Toronto: University of Toronto Press, 1962.

——. *Understanding Media: The Extensions of Man.* New York: Mentor Books, 1964.

——. *Understanding Media: The Extensions of Man.* Cambridge: MIT Press, 1994. 30th anniversary edition with a new introduction by Lewis Lapham.

Meyrowitz, Norman. "Does it Reduce Cholesterol, Too?" In Nyce and Kahn, eds. *From Memex to Hypertext.*

Minsky, Marvin. *The Society of Mind.* New York: Simon and Schuster, 1987.

Mitchell, William J. *City of Bits: Space, Place, and the Infobahn.* Cambridge, MA: MIT Press, 1995.

Moravec, Hans. *Mind Children: The Future of Robot and Human Intelligence.* Cambridge, MA: Harvard University Press, 1988.

Murray, Janet Horowitz. *Hamlet on the Holodeck: The Future of Narrative in Cyberspace.* New York: Free Press, 1997.

Negroponte, Nicholas. *Being Digital.* New York: Alfred A. Knopf, 1995.

——. *The Architecture Machine.* Cambridge: MIT, 1970.

Nelson, Theodor Holm. *Dream Machines.* Redmond, WA: Microsoft Press, 1987.

——. "Getting it Out of Our System." *Information Retrieval: A Critical Review.* G. Schechter, ed. Washington, DC: Thompson Books, 1967.

——. *Literary Machines, Edition 87.1 (The Report On, And Of, Project Xanadu Concerning Word Processing, Electronic Publishing, Hypertext, Thinkertoys, Tomorrow's Intellectual Revolution, And Certain Other Topics Including Knowledge, Education And Freedom).* Bellvue, WA: Microsoft Press, 1987.

——. "Managing Immense Storage." *Byte*, January 1988.

——. "Replacing the Printed Word: A Complete Literary System." *IFIP Proceedings*, October 1980, 1013-1023.

Nix, Don. "Should Computers Know What You Can Do With Them?" *Teachers College Record* 89, 3 (Spring 1988): 418-430.

Nyce, James M., and Paul Kahn, eds. *From Memex to Hypertext: Vannevar Bush and the Mind's Machine.* Boston: Academic Press, 1991.

O'Donell, James J., *Avatatrs of the Word: From Papyrus to Cyberspace.* Cambridge: Harvard University Press, 1998.

Ong, Walter. *Orality and Literacy: The Technologizing of the Word.* London: Metheun, 1982.

Orwell, George. *1984.* New York: Signet Library, 1961.

Pagels, Heinz R. *The Deams of Reason: The Computer and the Rise of the Sciences of Complexity.* New York: Bantam Books, 1989.

Palladio, Andrea. *The Four Books of Architecture.* With a new introduction by Adolf K. Placzek. New York: Dover Publications, 1965. Reprint of a 1738 edition of Palladio's work published in English and based on a 1570 Italian edition of the work.

Paz, Octavio. "The New Analogy: Poetry and Technology." In *Convergence: Essays on Art and Literature.* Translated from the Spanish by Helen Lane. San Diego: Harcourt Brace Jovanovich, 1987.

Peterson, Ivars. "Space-Time Odyssey: Visualizing the Effects of Traveling Near the Speed of Light," *Science News* Vol. 137 (April 14, 1990), 232.

Pool, Ithiel de Sola. *Technologies of Freedom: On Free Speech in an Electronic Age.* Cambridge: Harvard University Press, 1983.

Porter, David, ed. *Internet Culture.* New York: Routledge, 1997.

Provenzo, Eugene F., Jr. *Beyond the Gutenberg Galaxy: Microcomputers and the Emergence of Post-Typographic Culture.* New York: Teachers College Press, 1986.

——. "The Electronic Panopticon: Censorship, Control and Indoctrination in a Post-Typographic Culture." In Myron Tuman, ed. *Literacy Online: The Promise (and Peril) of Reading and Writing with Computers.* Pittsburgh: University of Pittsburgh Press, 1992, 167-178.

Purves, Alan. *The Web of Text and the Web of God: An Essay on the Third Information Transformation.* New York: Guilford Press, 1998.

Rheingold, Howard. *Tools for Thought: The People and Ideas Behind the Next Computer Revolution.* New York: Simon and Schuster, 1985.

Richtin, Fred. *In Our Image: The Coming Revolution in Photography.* New York: Aperture, 1990. Second Edition 1999.

Robins, Natalie. "The F. B. I.'s Invasion of Libraries," *The Nation,* April 9, 1988, 498-502.

Ryan, Steve, et al. *The Virtual University: The Internet and Resource-Based Learning.* London: Kogan Page, 2000.

Seal-Wanner, Carla. "Interactive Video Systems: Their Promises and Educational Potential." *Teachers College Record* 89, 3 (Spring 1988): 373-383.

Serlio, Sebastiano. *The Five Books of Architecture.* New York: Dover Publications, 1968. Reprint of a 1611 English edition of the work first published in 1537.

Slouka, Mark. *War of the Worlds: Cyberspace and the High-Tech Assault on Reality.* New York: Basic Books, 1995.

Sterne, Laurence. *The Life and Opinions of Tristram Shandy, Gentleman.* Boston: Houghton-Mifflin Company, 1965.

Stinchcombe, Arthur L. "Social Structure and Organizations." In James G. March, ed. *Handbook of Organizations.* Chicago: Rand McNally, 1965, 142-260.

Streitfield, David. "Credit Card Firm Says It's Their Privilege." *The Miami Herald,* May 6, 1989.

Talbot, Stephen L. *The Future Does Not Compute: Transcending the Machines In Our Midst.* Sebastopol: CA: O'Reilly & Associates, Inc., 1995.

Taylor, Todd, and Irene Ward, eds. *Literacy Theory in the Age of the Internet.* New York: Columbia University Press, 1998.

Thompson, James Westfall. *Ancient Libraries.* Berkeley: University of California Press, 1940.

Tiffin, John and Lalita Rajasingham. *The Global Virtual University.* New York: RoutledgeFalmer, 2003.

Tuman, Myron C., ed. *Literacy Online: The Promise (and Peril) of Reading and Writing with Computers.* Pittsburgh: University of Pittsburgh Press, 1992.

Turkle, Sherry. *Life on the Screen: Identity in the Age of the Internet.* New York: Simon & Schuster, 1995.

Van White, Jan. *Graphic Design for the Electronic Age: The Manual for Traditional and Desktop Publishing.* New York: Waton-Guptill Publications, 1988.

Vinge, Vernor. *True Names . . . and Other Dangers.* New York: Baen Books, 1989.

Vredeman de Vries, Jan. *Perspective.* With a new introduction by Adolf K. Placzek. New York: Dover Publications, 1968. Reprint of a 1604 edition.

Weizenbaum, Joseph. *Computer Power and Human Reason.* San Francisco: W. H. Freeman and Company, 1976.

Wiener, Norbert. *The Human Use of Human Beings: Cybernetics and Society.* New York: Avon Books, 1967.

Wilde, Candee. "The Internet & Electronic Commerce: A Revolution Begins." *The New York Times,* March 24, 1996.

Wilkins, John. *An Essay Towards a Real Character and a Philosophical Language* (London, 1668). Reprint, ed. by R. C. Alston, English Linguistics 1500-1800. Menston, England: Scolar Press, 1968.

Wills, Gary. Review of *Jefferson's Literary Commonplace Book* (ed. by Douglas L. Wilson). *The New Republic*, January 22, 1990.

Winograd, Terry, and Fernando Flores. *Understanding Computers and Cognition*. Reading, MA: Addison Wesley Publishing Company, 1987.

Yankelovich, N., N. Meyrowitz, and A. van Dam. "Reading and Writing the Electronic Book," *Computer*, October 1985.

Young, Robert. *A Critical Theory of Education: Habermas and Our Children's Future*. New York: Teachers College Press, 1990.

Zimmer, Carl. "Floppy Fiction." *Discover*, November 1989.

Zuboff, Shoshana. *In the Age of the Smart Machine: The Future of Work and Power*. New York: Basic Books, 1988.

Index

About the Author

Eugene F. Provenzo Jr. is a Professor of Education at the University of Miami. Trained as an historian of education he has been interested throughout his career in issues relating to the impact of technology on education and learning. His books *Beyond the Gutenberg Galaxy: Microcomputers and the Emergence of Post-Typographic Culture* (New York: Teachers College Press, Columbia University, 1986) and *Video Kids: Making Sense of Nintendo* (Cambridge, MA: Harvard University Press, 1991) are widely considered pioneering works in computing education, literacy and culture. In December, 1993 he testified before the United States Senate joint hearing of the Judiciary Subcommittee on Juvenile Justice and the Government Affairs Subcommittee on Regulation and Government Information on the issue of violence in video games and television, and in March, 2000 before the Senate Transportation and Commerce Committee on issues of children and interactive technology. In the spring of 2008 he was awarded the University of Miami's Provost's Award for Scholarly Activity.